WITHDRAWN

William Benke
Le Etta Benke

Church Wake-Up Call
A Ministries Management Approach That Is Purpose-Oriented and Inter-Generational in Outreach

Pre-publication
REVIEWS,
COMMENTARIES,
EVALUATIONS . . .

"**B**ill and Le Etta, in my review, turn out to be a 'winning pair' in *Church Wake-Up Call*. Their book delivers a fresh new perspective for Christian organizations facing today's challenge of change.

We are fortunate that Bill, one of the aerospace industry's top analytical problem solvers, and his talented wife, Le Etta, address the epic struggle of Christian churches to keep their ministries relevant in today's age-related cultural diversity. The new concepts they introduce provide an improved response to the spiritual void they sense is growing in the lives of the American people."

Malcolm Stamper
Publisher and CEO,
Storytellers, Ink;
Former Vice Chairman,
The Boeing Company,
Seattle, WA

More pre-publication
REVIEWS, COMMENTARIES, EVALUATIONS . . .

"**B**ill Benke combines personal integrity with an uncanny analytical capability. In the business world, his analytical mind has reached across multiple disciplines, including engineering, marketing, production, financial, and others, in addressing complex management problems. His solutions are always based upon pure analysis without political, social, or personal bias and his life focus reflects strong spiritual beliefs, another reason he is so well respected by his colleagues.

This book capably dissects a sensitive and important issue by combining business experience with a spiritual foundation, and provides unique insights into a major challenge that faces the church today, in terms of more effective ministries management."

Thomas J. Bacher
*President,
International Consulting Services,
Bellevue, WA*

"**M**any pastors are so close to the pew, they can't see the people.

Bill and Le Etta Benke have thoroughly analyzed the challenges of today's church culture, offering some hands-on, practical, and tested solutions. This book challenges an urgent response to the cries from the multigenerational church that are often being ignored. This compilation of resolutions is must reading for pastors and ministry workers desirous of investigating effective remedies for the needs of their congregations."

Reverend Wilbur James Antisdale
*Pastor Emeritus,
Westminster Chapel,
Bellevue, WA*

BEST BUSINESS BOOKS

Best Business Books
An Imprint of The Haworth Press, Inc.
New York • London • Oxford

NOTES FOR PROFESSIONAL LIBRARIANS
AND LIBRARY USERS

This is an original book title published by Best Business Books, an imprint of The Haworth Press, Inc. Unless otherwise noted in specific chapters with attribution, materials in this book have not been previously published elsewhere in any format or language.

CONSERVATION AND PRESERVATION NOTES

All books published by The Haworth Press, Inc. and its imprints are printed on certified pH neutral, acid free book grade paper. This paper meets the minimum requirements of American National Standard for Information Sciences-Permanence of Paper for Printed Material, ANSI Z39.48-1984.

Church Wake-Up Call
*A Ministries Management Approach
That Is Purpose-Oriented
and Inter-Generational in Outreach*

BEST BUSINESS BOOKS
Robert E. Stevens, PhD
David L. Loudon, PhD
Editors in Chief

Strategic Planning for Collegiate Athletics by Deborah A. Yow, R. Henry Migliore, William W. Bowden, Robert E. Stevens, and David L. Loudon

Church Wake-Up Call: A Ministries Management Approach That Is Purpose-Oriented and Inter-Generational in Outreach by William Benke and Le Etta N. Benke

Organizational Behavior by Jeff O. Harris and Sandra J. Hartman

Marketing Research Essentials: Text and Cases by W. Bruce Wrenn, Robert E. Stevens, and David L. Loudon

Doing Business in Mexico: A Practical Guide by Gus Gordon and Thurmon Williams

Church Wake-Up Call
*A Ministries Management Approach
That Is Purpose-Oriented
and Inter-Generational in Outreach*

William Benke
Le Etta Benke

BEST BUSINESS BOOKS

Best Business Books
An Imprint of The Haworth Press, Inc.
New York • London • Oxford

Published by

Best Business Books, an imprint of The Haworth Press, Inc., 10 Alice Street, Binghamton, NY 13904-1580

© 2001 by The Haworth Press, Inc. All rights reserved. No part of this work may be reproduced or utilized in any form or by any means, electronic or mechanical, including photocopying, microfilm, and recording, or by any information storage and retrieval system, without permission in writing from the publisher. Printed in the United States of America.

Scripture quotations marked (LB) are from *The Living Bible,* copyright ©1971, by Tyndale House Publishers, P.O. Box 80, Wheaton, IL 60289. Used by permission of Tyndale House Publishers. All rights reserved. Scripture quotations marked (NIV) are taken from the HOLY BIBLE, NEW INTERNATIONAL VERSION®. Copyright ©1973, 1978, 1984 by International Bible Society. Used by permission of Zondervan Publishing House. All rights reserved. Scripture quotations marked (KJV) are from the King James Version of the Bible.

Cover design by Marylouise E. Doyle.

Library of Congress Cataloging-in-Publication Data

Benke, William, 1927-
   Church wake-up call : a ministries management approach that is purpose-oriented and intergenerational in outreach / William Benke, Le Etta Benke.
      p. cm.
   Includes bibliographical references and index.
   ISBN 0-7890-1137-9 (alk. paper) — ISBN 0-7890-1138-7 (soft : alk. paper)
   1. Church management. I. Benke, Le Etta. II. Title.

BV652 .B44 2000
254—dc21

00-031240

To Danielle, Dustin, Drew, and Kristel

ABOUT THE AUTHORS

William Benke is a former business executive with forty years of experience in the management of strategic and international business planning with such companies as Boeing, Coca-Cola, Montgomery Ward, and Welch's. Special assignments have included responsibility for corporate task force teams to address complex internal problems and policy direction. He is a graduate of New York University with a degree in administrative engineering. His broad analytical skills extend to real estate investment management, the subject of three of his books, as well as to a variety of civic/community volunteer activities. He has been called upon to render specialized organizational, management, and planning assistance to such civic programs as the Seattle Opera, the Seattle Art Museum, the King Tutankhamen exhibit when it appeared in Seattle, Childhaven (rehabilitates abused and neglected children), the Salvation Army, and Storytellers, Ink (a not-for-profit corporation that instills moral values in children through books on animal stories). He is also an active Christian layman, having served on the boards of both small and megasized churches, local Child Evangelism Fellowship organizations, and several Christian camping ministries. He also has authored articles for Christian periodicals on church organization and child evangelism.

Le Etta Benke has been a legal secretary and research specialist and assists in all of these projects. She, too, has a substantial commercial background and, although retired, currently chairs the supervisory board of a major regional credit union and has held important administrative responsibilities with church organizations. The Benkes work together as a uniquely effective husband and wife team.

CONTENTS

Preface	ix
Chapter 1. Introduction and Overview	1
Chapter 2. The Market	9
The Baby Boomers	11
Generation X (Baby Busters)	19
The Youth	22
The Pre-Boomers	24
Ministry Implications	28
Chapter 3. Priorities	33
Child Evangelism	33
Youth Evangelism	40
Adult Evangelism	42
Church Size	46
Community Service or Assistance	48
Chapter 4. A Word About Management	59
Chapter 5. Purposes	65
The Ministries Matrix	75
Chapter 6. Using the Ministries Matrix	79
Getting Organized	79
The Leadership Council	81
Setting Priorities	82
Recording Current Programming on the Ministries Matrix	86
Evaluating the Current Ministries Plan	91
Chapter 7. Developing a Ministries Strategy	97
Multigenerational Centralized Strategy	97
Targeted Centralized Strategy	98

Small Groups Strategy	99
Satellite Churches	100
House Church Strategy	102
Traditional and Contemporary Services Strategy	103
Grace Church Strategy	104
Other Follow-Up Activities	107

Chapter 8. Visibility — 111

Evangelism Visibility	112
Growth Visibility	112
Discipleship Visibility	112
Generational Visibility	113

Chapter 9. Organization — 115

Organization by Function	115
Organization by Age	118
Ministries Oversight and Interface	119

Chapter 10. The Challenge of Change — 123

Notes — 127

Recommended Reading — 131

Index — 135

Preface

In case you have not noticed, we are in the midst of a revolution—cultural, that is! America has undergone major cultural change during the past decade or two, and there is more to come. The change is generationally oriented and began a little over thirty years ago when the Baby Boomers entered the scene as adults. They ushered in a new cultural paradigm for their generation and a challenge to traditional values and Christian influence. This was exacerbated by the generation that followed, Generation X or Baby Busters, who entered the scene as adults about fifteen years ago with a significantly different cultural orientation and further skepticism about the church, born largely out of the influence and erosion in family structure that the Boomers introduced. The next generational wave, currently in youth status but on the verge of adulthood, is showing evidence that it will bring along its own attitudes and cultural characteristics. Meanwhile, the Pre-Boomers, who are either entering or are well into senior status, are still on the scene; they are living longer and are of an entirely different cultural ilk than the generations that have succeeded them.

All of this equates to an unprecedented challenge for the church. It needs to minister to a multigenerational/multicultural society. Unfortunately, a major disconnect lies in the typical church's ability to adapt to change and the rate of societal change that now exists. One of the major problems is an antiquated concept of ministries management that is unable to respond effectively to the complexity of today's multigenerational challenge. In terms of management methodology, the church has simply not kept pace with the rest of the organizational world. Many excellent books are available on church ministries that focus on church problems, the implications of changing societal trends, and programs or ministry concepts to address these issues. Noticeably lacking is the management aspect, reflecting the fact that most books on ministries or church outreach are written by pastors, theology scholars, or members of academia, many of whom lack significant business management experience. This is not a criticism. It is simply an occupational reality. Moreover, ministries-oriented professionals are people-oriented by nature, as well they should be. Management methods, systems, and processes are neither their life interest nor is it an area to which they can afford to devote a great deal of time, yet still excel in their primary focus. However, this missing ingredient, effective ministries management, may well be the Achilles' heel of the church in today's environment of dynamic change. A major transfusion of know-how and application of modern practice is needed if the church is to keep pace and remain relevant in people's lives.

Churches that persist in outdated ministry paradigms and fail to adapt to the current generation-based multicultural environment are destined to become antiquated relics. Those that accept the challenge of change and gear up through effective management methods to respond to this challenge face the prospect of spiritual reward and success. Statistics reveal the existence of a great spiritual void that awaits fulfillment in the lives of many Americans. Unlocking the key to this large market requires a transition to new methods and ministry approaches, and a management discipline that causes this to happen.

This book will not turn you into a management expert. However, it will help in some small but strategically important way by introducing some basic principles and an easy-to-implement management process. This process can transform the local church from drifting along in a well-intentioned but inefficient and unresponsive manner to a directed approach that integrates purposes, priorities, and ministries through a well-coordinated plan of action. Nothing less would be acceptable to the secular corporation if it is to survive and prosper in today's competitive and changing world. Should we expect less from the church?

Although this book is oriented toward churches and their leadership and has been written largely from an evangelical Christian perspective, the characteristics describing each of the several generational categories that comprise today's populace are relevant and applicable to all Christian organizations, whether they are evangelical or mainline Protestant, Catholic, or parachurch. Such characteristics describe the "market," regardless of doctrinal persuasion or the specific religious body involved, and must be properly understood and accommodated if defined purposes of the organization are to be achieved. Similarly, the management system, which integrates defined purposes, priorities, and programming options into a well-coordinated plan of action, can be applied by all such organizations. Although the purposes and programming or ministry options may differ significantly for each, the management system described is designed to accommodate such input differences.

Chapter 1

Introduction and Overview

The scene is a familiar one. The church board is meeting with the Building Committee to consider the recommendations from that committee on the proposed Christian education building. The committee presents a thorough and well-written report complete with architectural drawings, cost estimates, financing options, and a construction timetable. The excitement heightens as the pastor endorses the project and encourages the board to approve the plan.

The board votes unanimously to "take this step of faith." Immediately the Building Committee goes into action. A congregational kick-off meeting is held. Plans are made to make personal visits to each member's home to communicate the building plans and solicit pledges. A huge "thermometer" display, which is updated weekly, is erected in a corner of the social hall, showing the financial progress of raising the needed funds or commitments. A careful search is made for the general contractor who will do the best work at the lowest price. Subcontractor bids are reviewed, related negotiations carried out, and contracts signed. The maze of local government permits, environmental impact statements, and other regulatory paperwork is eventually accomplished and the necessary approvals are obtained. Financing arrangements are worked out with the lending institution, and community meetings are held to answer questions and allay fears that the building program will cause neighborhood disruption and traffic problems. The local newspapers are alerted and somehow men and women freely give of their time to attend long evening meetings to work out the thousands of details associated with a building program. God blesses, it seems, and there is a collective enthusiasm and commitment of purpose that soon converts plans, financial targets, contracts, and schedule deadlines into realities. In time, the building is completed. A dedication service is held with denominational dignitaries—and then the pastor and his church leaders return home to get reacquainted with their families!

Another scene is just as familiar. It is the monthly church board meeting that carries out routine oversight functions of the church. The typical focus of these meetings centers on verbal reports by leaders concerning various ministry areas, with the primary purpose of addressing problems, decisions, and approvals that rise to the church board level of responsibility or authority. It also deals with unusual spiritual problems or congregational needs that may surface. The underlying philosophy is to leave well enough alone if things are running smoothly, and to focus primarily on problems and nonroutine situations. Except when problem issues or special situations arise (such as the new building program), the collective wisdom can be summed up in those well-known adages, "Don't rock the boat," and "If it ain't broke, don't fix it." This philosophy of the status quo has the tendency to delay decisive action until programs become moribund and ministry rigor mortis begins to set in. In today's environment of dramatic societal change, this management style is a formula for stagnation and decline.

The paradox between these two scenes suggests that often different management styles exist for different types of church functions. One is the general *administrative* functions, such as financial management, recordkeeping, capital expansions, building and grounds maintenance, secretarial and clerical support, and other similar overhead functions that provide the setting or environment for the church to operate. The other major category is *church ministries*. This refers to all of the programs that, in one way or another, reach out to, communicate with, or serve people in the church and community. The two different scenes described demonstrate how two different management styles often prevail over each category. A *proactive* approach, such as that described for the Building Committee, is frequently the case for the administrative category or special projects. The ministries category, however, tends to be characterized in many churches by a *reactive* approach (reaction to problems), such as that described for the church board meeting, where maintaining status quo and persistence in an outdated ministry paradigm is the norm.

Imagine what might happen if the church board adopted the management style of the Building Committee in the current environment of cultural change in which churches must adapt to new ministry approaches if they are to remain vibrant and relevant. One in which programs and ministries were critically reviewed, planned, financed, approached with enthusiasm toward well-defined purposes, and then monitored in terms of compliance, as was the building program. The impact on the non-Christian community would likely be quite dramatic. Unfortunately, churches often fall into a pattern of running ministries based on tradition rather than on current relevance.

In many respects, the church board is to the church what the board of directors is to the commercial corporation. However, there is one glaring difference. The primary focus of the corporate board of directors is on a single bottom-line criterion—profitability. Almost everything, directly or indirectly, revolves around this key index. Expected financial results are either achieved or serious attention is promptly directed toward changes to programs or personnel, or possibly both. The stockholders demand such action.

Most churches do not have such a "bottom-line" mentality when it comes to ministries. But they can and should. A bottom-line approach for churches, however, must center on their spiritual purposes. This is the subject of Chapter 5. For most churches, these purposes have to do with evangelism, discipleship, worship, fellowship, mutual caring, community service, and other people-oriented outreaches. But how can such considerations be translated into a "bottom line" that provides the basis for monitoring, evaluating, redirecting, canceling, revitalizing, or replacing current programs or ministries, as appropriate? Some individual ministries lend themselves to the use of statistical measures of performance, and this is addressed elsewhere. But the effectiveness of the church ministry as a whole cannot be reduced to a single statistical index in the way that is possible for commercial corporations. However, church ministries can be reviewed periodically in terms of their individual and collective effectiveness to the "bottom-line" spiritual purposes of the church and the relative priorities of those purposes. For example, if, after a process in which the church's purposes (the reason for which it exists) are clearly defined and prioritized, it is determined that evangelism is a top purpose and priority, then the orientation and focus of an appropriate number of programs ought to be geared toward that end, and new converts should be the result. If an evaluation of program ministries reveals otherwise, there is an obvious problem. Namely, an imbalance exists between the desired spiritual emphasis—the "bottom-line" purposes of the church and its relative priorities—and the way the church is utilizing its people and resources. The corrective action called for may be to reorient certain programs or ministries, launch new ones, or possibly cancel and replace others in order to bring evangelistic outreach back into proper balance.

Sounds simple enough. But in reality a wide divergence will often be found between the typical programs that collectively comprise the total church ministry and the spiritual purposes for which it exists, once they have been properly defined. Part of the problem is that most churches never get around to defining in specific terms the purposes and the program objectives into which purposes must ultimately be translated. Often programs and ministries are sustained because they have always been done that way. They become institutionalized on the basis of time and tradition and are never critically reviewed or challenged as to current relevancy. It is like the proverbial frog placed in cool water that is gradually heated until it reaches a boil, and the poor frog ends up cooked without realizing the gradual change in environment that led to its demise.

Another corollary is the traditional Sunday 11:00 a.m. worship hour, even though this time slot was apparently originally selected to accommodate farmers who needed to milk their cows before attending church. No criticism is intended concerning the 11:00 a.m. worship hour. The intent is simply to illustrate that choosing 11:00 a.m. as the best time ought to be based on today's considerations rather than when cows need milking. We fall into these "ministry ruts" based on past tradition rather than current relevancy, and the result can be very negative. This tendency is reinforced by our natural human inclination to resist change.

The role of church leadership in evaluating, monitoring, and assuring programs that fulfill its spiritual purposes is essential if the church is to adapt to societal changes that in recent decades have been quite dramatic. During the past twenty-five years or so, the Baby Boomers (those born from 1946 to 1964) have been the dominant influence in American society and in recent cultural changes. Coming to the forefront today is Generation X or the Baby Busters (those born from 1965 to 1984) and the youth generation, and with them further changes in attitudes, values, and cultural influences. The cultural changes being ushered in through these generational groups, the nature and implications of which are discussed in later chapters, are dramatic and must be accommodated in a positive way if the church is to remain relevant. In this cultural transition, a significant portion of the population has bought in to the new worldview of postmodernism. In this viewpoint, philosophical relativism is embraced and, since it rejects scriptural authority, no absolute truths or moral standards exist, at least none that we are capable of establishing or grasping. This philosophical shift has ushered in the trend toward religious pluralism, sexual perversion, and increasing violence—even among children, as schools replace the teaching of traditional values with postmodernist philosophy, the devaluation of human life, and increasing opposition to Judeo-Christian ethics based upon biblical truth. With these societal changes comes the need for ministry changes. Determining the appropriate nature of such changes is complicated because we live in a multicultural rather than a culturally monolithic society. "Multicultural" is used here in the context of differences between the four generational categories referred to, namely, Youth, Generation X, Baby Boomers, and Pre-Boomers. Multiculturalism, or cultural diversity, also exists today in terms of racial, ethnic, and other considerations that are not generation based. This other aspect of multiculturalism is not the focus of this book. Generational multiculturalism transcends other cultural differences in that all racial and ethnic groups also embody the generation-based cultural dimensions.

The ministry of the church must be structured to accommodate these considerations and communicate the Christian message to all generational categories. This may imply different methods of interface and communication to each. But it does not imply the need to compromise the message. Culture changes but God does not. We do not have to be shaped by our culture, but we will find it increasingly necessary to exchange comfortable familiarities for new approaches that are better adapted to the change.

The challenge before the church today is greater than it has ever been. Although surveys differ somewhat in their findings, it appears that as many as 60 percent of all American adults do not currently attend church on a consistent basis. With an adult population of about 200 million, this equates to roughly 120 million adults who do not attend church regularly, compared with about 80 million who do. Surveys by George Barna's research organization indicate that only about half of all churchgoers are born-again Christians and, of those who do not attend regularly, about 17 percent are trusting Christ alone for salvation.[1] Based on these statistics and a little arithmetic, the picture depicted by the Exhibit 1.1 matrix emerges and suggests the following:

1. Seventy percent of American adults are not born-again Christians and, as indicated above, about 60 percent are unchurched. This translates into a huge mission field and outreach challenge to the church.
2. Since 10 percent of Americans do not regularly attend church but are professing Christians, the church apparently is failing to effectively minister to the needs of a large segment of believers.
3. Since 20 percent of Americans attend church but are not Christians, they are either involved in churches that do not proclaim an evangelical Christian message or the message is not getting across. In either case, this segment also represents a huge outreach opportunity.

The purpose of this book is to provide some simple but effective techniques and principles for church leaders interested in considering a more systematic and *proactive* church management style to meet this challenge of change, as opposed to the more informal *reactive* emphasis that is often the norm. It is intended as a tool for reflective thinking, group discussion, and sharing by local church leaders as they contemplate where they want to take their church in the days and years ahead. By design, the book is relatively short, easy to read, and the basic ideas for church planning and oversight are quite simple. But sometimes the simple, and what becomes the obvious, once recognized, needs to be called to our attention since,

EXHIBIT 1.1. The Market Challenge

	EVANGELICAL CHRISTIANS	OTHERS	
ATTEND CHURCH REGULARLY	20% (1/2 × 40%)	20% (1/2 × 40%)	40%
DO NOT ATTEND CHURCH REGULARLY	10% (17% × 60%)	50% (83% × 60%)	60%
	30%	70%	

as the old adage goes, "We lose sight of the forest for the trees." This book seeks to stimulate those in church leadership roles to take a fresh look at things in an objective way that may lead to some creative thinking and new strategies for ministries that will help steer their church to new heights in terms of fulfilling its mission.

Such a fresh look, along with the techniques outlined in this book, are believed to offer the potential of stirring the same degree of enthusiasm, energy, and expertise that we experience in building programs and other administrative functions to the areas of evangelism, discipleship, mutual support and encouragement, and other spiritual outreach ministries. These ministries, after all, also constitute a building program. "[W]e will in all things grow up into him who is the Head, that is, Christ. From him the whole body, joined and held together by every supporting ligament, grows and builds itself up in love, as each part does its work" (Ephesians 4:15-16 NIV).

The next two chapters focus on the market and information concerning ministry priorities that appear to be relevant in this market. The balance of the book then addresses a ministries management process, which is designed for use by churches in establishing a purpose-oriented ministries program.

A brief word to those in the ministry. Because you are people and program oriented, you will likely be much more comfortable with the first part of the book that deals with the market and ministries than with the latter part that focuses on a management process. But this process is a vital missing ingredient in the church today in terms of establishing a dynamic structured plan for a total ministry that responds to well-thought-out purposes, once these purposes are clearly defined. It involves a thought process that is lacking in the church today, largely because spiritual leaders are not usually business oriented and also because seminaries and Bible schools do not teach Management 101. But the local church is a human organization, and to function effectively it needs to adopt many of the same time-proven management methods that commercial corporations employ. So please take the time to understand the process, and then the portion of the book that deals with people and ministries will take on added significance as they are viewed in the context of a structured total plan.

Chapter 2

The Market

Effective use of any ministries management system begins with an understanding of the market, namely the population to which the church seeks to minister. In describing this market, we have relied upon those much more knowledgeable than ourselves on the subject and refer frequently to their findings and writings. Our purpose is to provide an overview perspective of the market, as well as a synopsis of the key characteristics of its several components. This is foundational to evaluating current ministries and the development of a ministries plan, the primary focus of this book and the subject of later chapters.

The market consists of several generational categories: Children, Youth, Generation X (born from 1965 to 1984), the Baby Boomers (born from 1946 to 1964), and the Pre-Boomers (born prior to 1946). The Pre-Boomers can be further categorized as the Builders (born from 1927 to 1945) and the Blazers (born before 1926). Exhibit 2.1 illustrates the adult generational categories in terms of the age-range of each in the year 2000.

As noted in Exhibit 2.2, using 1997 data, the Boomers represent the largest segment, about 29 percent, of the total population.[1] This generation is particularly significant, not only in terms of population size, but because it has ushered in major cultural changes. These changes have, in turn, impacted the generation that followed, Generation X, to create yet another culture. Generation Xers rival the Boomers in population size, representing about 28 percent of the total population. At the heels of Generation X is the Youth category. In fact, the older youth are a part of Generation X. In total, Youth (ages 13-18) represent about 8.5 percent of the population, but two-thirds of these are included in the Generation X category.

EXHIBIT 2.1. Age Range in Year 2000

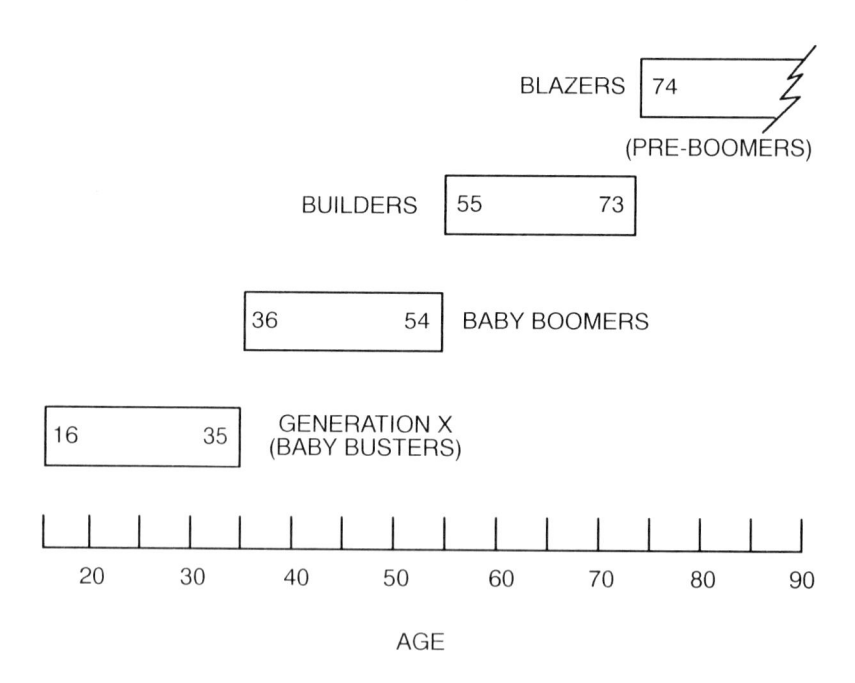

```
                                    BLAZERS  | 74      /|
                                             |_____/
                                             (PRE-BOOMERS)

                        BUILDERS  | 55        73 |

                   | 36        54 |  BABY BOOMERS

        | 16    35 |  GENERATION X
                     (BABY BUSTERS)

   |____|____|____|____|____|____|____|____|
   20   30   40   50   60   70   80   90
                    AGE
```

Children (ages 6-12) make up about 10 percent of the total. The Pre-Boomers and the Blazers, those over age fifty-five in the year 2000, account for about 24 percent of the population. The over-fifty-five age category is the fastest growing age segment (Exhibit 2.3). These statistics make it clear that the church will face a real challenge over the next decade. These different age groups or generations—the Baby Boomers, the Generation Xers that followed, along with the Youth nipping at their heels, and the Pre-Boomers of an earlier era—are all distinctly different in terms of their needs, values, ethics, and cultural orientation. These generational groups are discussed in that order, rather than in an age sequence, to provide a better perspective concerning where we are today culturally, how we got here, and the implications in terms of future ministries.

EXHIBIT 2.2. 1997 U.S. Population Distribution

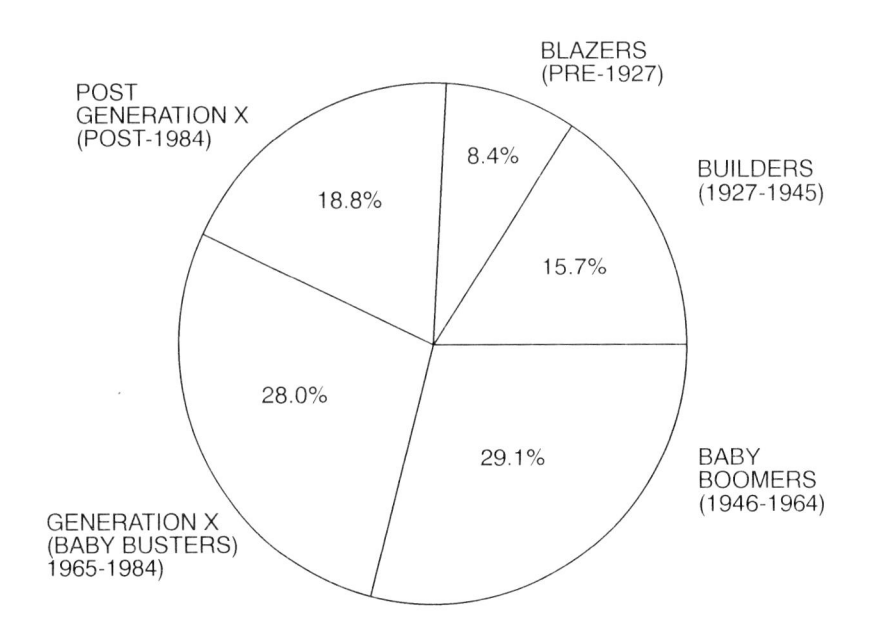

- BLAZERS (PRE-1927): 8.4%
- BUILDERS (1927-1945): 15.7%
- BABY BOOMERS (1946-1964): 29.1%
- GENERATION X (BABY BUSTERS) 1965-1984): 28.0%
- POST GENERATION X (POST-1984): 18.8%

Source: *Statistical Abstract of the United States: 1998,* Table No. 16, p. 16, U.S. Census Bureau.

THE BABY BOOMERS

When World War II (1941-1945) ended, a period of tranquility and an expanding economy followed, along with an unprecedented upsurge in the birth rate (Exhibit 2.4). Initially, this was attributed to soldiers returning home, being reunited with their families, and marriages taking place that had been deferred because of the war. But the birth upsurge continued for about twenty years, creating a population wave that has precipitated a succession of changes in American society and which will continue to do so for years to come. Futurists Ken Dychtwald and Joe Flower describe some of the unfolding impacts in their book, *Age Wave.*[2] At the infancy stage,

EXHIBIT 2.3. Percent Change in Population by Age: 2000 vs. 2010

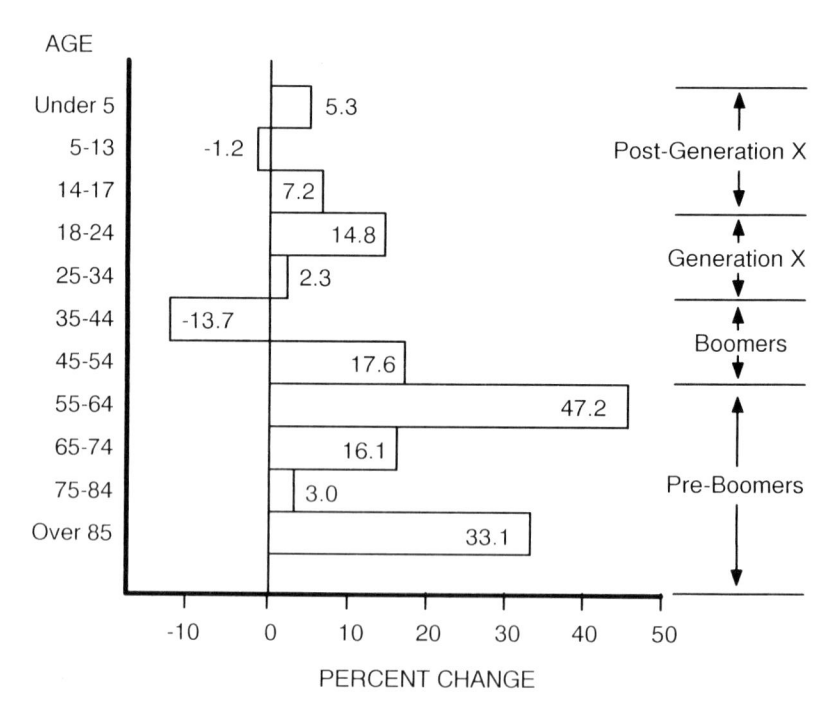

Age	Percent Change	Generation
Under 5	5.3	Post-Generation X
5-13	-1.2	Post-Generation X
14-17	7.2	Generation X
18-24	14.8	Generation X
25-34	2.3	Generation X
35-44	-13.7	Boomers
45-54	17.6	Boomers
55-64	47.2	Pre-Boomers
65-74	16.1	Pre-Boomers
75-84	3.0	Pre-Boomers
Over 85	33.1	Pre-Boomers

Source: Statistical Abstract of the United States: 1998, Table No. 24, p. 25, U.S. Census Bureau.

Boomers caused pediatric issues to come to the fore, and baby-based industries such as baby food and baby photos prospered. When the Boomers reached school age, they caused a school shortage and more elementary schools were built than in any prior year or since. Industries producing kids' toys and school supplies had a heyday and teachers' colleges had a big upswing in enrollment. At the teenage level, the high schoolers doubled between 1950 and 1975. High school construction increased, and industries and businesses catering to teenagers boomed, including soft drinks, records, movies, fast foods, and cosmetics. When they reached college age, they precipitated fierce entrance competition and the expansion of colleges. Student enrollment rose from 3.2 million in 1965 to 9 million

EXHIBIT 2.4. Live Births

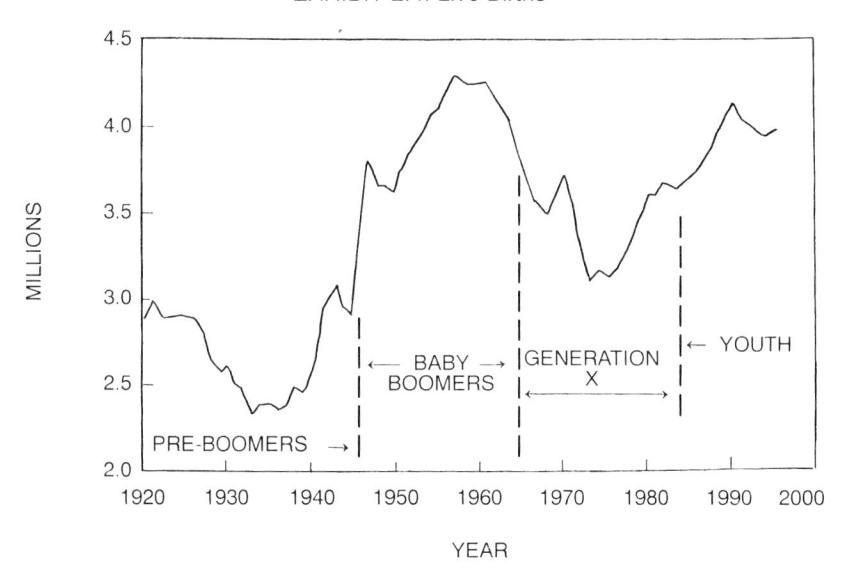

Source: Statistical Abstract of the United States: 1998, Table No. 92, p. 76, U.S. Census Bureau.

in 1975, and 743 new colleges opened. As the last Boomers graduated, a surplus of college capacity followed. In the 1970s, as the Boomers reached their twenties, they became concerned about personal identity, giving rise to such movements as Transcendental Meditation and Silva Mind Control. During the 1980s they reached the thirties age bracket, moved into the job market, and turned their focus to careers and families. Day care became an important issue and the "Yuppies" became a new part of the American scene. As the oldest Boomers now approach or enter retirement age, other major societal impacts are becoming evident, including those related to the financing of Social Security, the health care system, nursing homes, retirement facilities, financial and consumer markets, as well as the focus of church ministries.

Phrases or adjectives often used to describe the Boomers include results-oriented, live-to-work (as opposed to work-to-live), self-fulfillment, manipulative, idealistic, flashy, headstrong, low institutional loyalty, high expectations, ambitious to make the world better through political action, weaker relationships, get-ahead focus, career-oriented, and WIFM (what's in it for me) attitude. In his book *Bridge Over Troubled Water*,[3] James Bell summarizes the unique aspects of this generation:

> In stark contrast to the complexity of contemporary North American society, life in the pre-Boom days was rather simple. The significance of the family unit, the church, and the state were clearly recognized. Values were generally honored and recognized as essential for maintaining the common good. As the postwar Boomer generation began to evolve through its unique life cycle and establish its autonomy, it found itself in conflict with the values of its parents in the '60s. Events both at home and abroad caused them to experience an identity crisis, a widespread distrust in government, and a disregard for the church. Instead of viewing themselves as one generation interlocked with the preceding one, they tried to forge a new way of living where justice and peace would prevail and civil liberties would be honored. Eventually discouraged by the slowness of change, many Baby Boomers, perplexed and bewildered, withdrew to a hippie counter-culture that was more passive than the political activism of the '60s, or they set their sights on education and establishing career goals. In the '80s Baby Boomers re-emerged on the scene, this time driven almost obsessively in the pursuit of health, wealth, and happiness. By the '90s some had achieved financial success while others had not. But the one thing they did have in common was middle age. Now Baby Boomers are showing an interest in family life and basic values, and in the quest for meaning they are returning to occupy those absent pews that they left decades ago. (©1993 Cook Communications Ministries. *Bridge Over Troubled Water* by James Bell. Used with permission. May not be further reproduced. All rights reserved.)

Some general characteristics of this generation, discussed in much greater depth by Leith Anderson in *Dying for Change*[4] include:

- *Low loyalty:* This goes for brand name products as well as institutions, including the church. It explains the decline of churches that have not responded to the perceived needs of Baby Boomers and the shift from denominational labels to more responsive nondenominational churches.
- *Nonaffiliation:* Closely related, many Boomer church attendees do not become members. There is a willingness to switch churches based on need. Boomers tend to trust individuals more than institutions, making them more loyal to a specific minister than to a church or denomination.
- *High expectations:* Having grown up with a sense of entitlement, Boomers have high expectations from institutions. The implications are that churches that target Baby Boomers will flourish if they provide quality programs and facilities but do not require blind loyalty. This attitude of high expectations probably accounts for the high divorce and depression rates among Boomers as they experience disappointments and unmet expectations.
- *Weaker relationships:* Boomers are weak in building strong relationships. Related factors include high mobility and high divorce rates. Many successful churches have responded with the small group movement to address various needs. Examples include groups for adult children of alcoholics, athletic teams, music groups, parenting classes, employment services, cancer support, and Bible study.
- *Tolerance for diversity:* Boomers are very tolerant of individual differences and alternative lifestyles. This does not mean they do not have firm convictions, but they accept those with contrary convictions.
- *Comfortable with change:* Rapid and profound changes of the twentieth century have made change normal to Boomers. Churches that seek to avoid change and guarantee orthodoxy through rules and regulations find their efforts futile. Alternatively, some older leaders refuse to relinquish control to Baby Boomers because they fear Boomers will implement unwanted changes. Such churches are destined to die with the older membership.

- *Different leadership style:* Whether or not Boomers have a different leadership style may be debatable. They are inclined to be more participative, democratic, and attuned to employee needs. However, in reality, leaders tend to be mentored, groomed, and molded into conformity by those over them. Regardless, Boomers perceive themselves to be different. They create a sense of generational solidarity, pushing older leaders out and running operations differently. Churches and religious organizations are not exempt. Unless Boomers are integrated into leadership roles, defection or institutional conflict can be expected.
- *Different motivating values:* Unlike their parents, Boomers are motivated more by experiencing life than by materialism. Variety, risk, and change take precedence over job security and stability.
- *Seeking meaning:* Boomers appear to be searchers committed to finding a meaningful philosophy of life, although they have little faith in God. Churches seeking to relate to them will need amenities such as modern nursery facilities and good programs for children.

As a generation with high expectations and having been raised in an era of great scientific achievement, Boomers expect no less from the church. This means quality programs and facilities and may account in large measure for the trend toward "full service" churches. We live in an age when the small is giving way to the large. Small grocery stores have become largely extinct because of supermarkets. Neighborhood hardware stores are becoming a rarity as huge building supplies megastores take over. The same is true for sporting goods, appliances and home electronics, pet supplies, bookstores, and many other retailers. This is also happening to the church as more and more Americans are opting for full-service churches that offer quality and variety in such things as music, various types of support groups, diverse educational opportunities, multiple worship services, modern child care, athletic activities, extensive youth programs, singles ministries, a counseling staff, a large support base that reduces the obligation for personal involvement and commitment, and many other features available only in large churches. Although seeming to contradict the Boomer attitude of antiloyalty to institutions, they expect the excellence and choice offered by large full-service churches.

Incidentally, this trend toward larger churches is not all bad. Apart from responding to Boomer expectations of excellence and their sense of entitlement, it is also free market economics in operation. In many ways, a better product (ministries) for consumers (attendees) is provided and is done so on a more economical basis (contribution requirements). This is due to the economies of scale achieved as the fixed costs of operation (overhead, salaries, plant, and equipment, etc.) are allocated over a larger attendance basis, resulting in lower per capita costs. Nevertheless, this trend creates a problem for smaller churches.

Although the excellence of full-service churches is appealing to and expected by Boomers, they are most open to the message of Christ during times of personal crisis, suggesting the importance of small group workshop and support group ministries. Leith Anderson writes:[5]

> A word of caution, however: churches and Christian organizations will not effectively reach baby boomers with 1950 methods and programs. We must relate to boomers in terms of their distinctions and in response to their needs. Most won't just "show up" at a Sunday church service to hear the Gospel. They will be attracted by modern ministry facilities, excellent pre-schools, and attractive youth programs for their children. They will become open to the message of Jesus Christ during the transition times of their lives, such as divorce, remarriage, the birth of a child, unemployment, or the death of a parent. But that message will probably get through to them through a divorce recovery workshop, an unemployment support group, or a workshop on grief rather than through a sermon.

Programs that a number of mainstream churches have reported to be effective include:[6]

- *Parents' night out:* The church provides child care on a weekend evening. Professional sitters or preschool teachers are used.
- *Dial-a-children's story:* Children can call a special phone number to hear a three-minute recorded story, after which they are invited to attend Sunday school or a summer Bible program.

- *Single parent parking:* A sticker is provided that allows parking in special spaces convenient to the nursery.
- *Ministries that foster religious training and teaching values in the home:* One church publishes a weekly newsletter featuring a children's story for parents to use in teaching the Bible at home. Another provides cassette tapes that can be played while driving.
- *Small group ministries:* These center around a variety of lifestyle workshops or support groups, including divorce recovery, blended families, gamblers anonymous, unemployment, single parents, overeaters anonymous, engaged couples, young fathers, depression, parents of emotionally disabled children, etc.
- *Weekday ministries:* A variety of ministries are being implemented by some churches during weekday hours, such as preschool, Bible study, senior citizens, neighborhood groups, and small group ministries. Some have a major weekday event preceded by a quality meal.
- *Hands-on locally controlled mission projects:* These allow personal participation on a short-term basis. Examples are Habitat for Humanity and Vacation with a Purpose, in which small teams go to foreign mission fields for ten days to assist in a specific project. Personal spiritual growth is the goal.
- *Sport ministries:* Some churches develop extensive athletic ministries. One reports that 7 percent of the unchurched participants eventually join the church.
- *Transitional ministries:* The transitional characteristics of Boomer lifestyle (cohabitation, delayed childbirth, divorce, remarriage) create periods of responsiveness to invitations to attend church and provide opportunities to minister through support groups of the type mentioned earlier.
- *High-tech opportunities:* These include short videos to acquaint visitors with various ministries of the church; computers in Sunday school to motivate and facilitate learning scripture; Christian education software for computers; television ministries to shut-ins and hospital patients.
- *Women's ministry:* "How To" seminars on such subjects as balancing careers and home, parenting, values clarification, support groups for mothers, etc.

- *Quarterly Sunday school teachers:* Teachers sign up for three- to four-month commitments, instead of open-end obligations. This attracts more people willing to teach but has the problems of more teacher training and the fact that children prefer a familiar face. Many short-term teachers, however, accept longer-term commitments following the experience.
- *Retreat settings:* These enhance opportunities for personal interface, growth, and spiritual renewal.
- *Crisis ministries:* The Boomers' obsession with instant gratification makes them vulnerable to crisis situations (death, illness, job loss, special-needs child, divorce, etc.). Trained counselors are the key to this ministry.
- *Churchwide prayer ministries:* Intercessory prayer is encouraged concerning prayer requests received via receptacles at the entrance, registration cards, a prayer hotline, and the collection of names during Sunday school. Prayer chains and prayer teams that meet prior to the service also help Boomers look beyond themselves to others.

GENERATION X (BABY BUSTERS)

An excellent resource for understanding the Xers is *Generating Hope: A Strategy for Reaching the Postmodern Generation* by Jimmy Long.[7] His book draws upon experience as regional director of Intervarsity Christian Fellowship and pastor of a campus ministry for over twenty years. His book describes Generation X characteristics in depth and the implications for ministry. Following are some key points that Long and others point out concerning this generation.

Many are the offspring of the Baby Boomers and are gradually displacing them in terms of societal influences in decision making, leadership, and cultural direction. Studies concerning Generation X typically characterize them as being confused, feeling hopeless, unfocused, skeptical, uncommitted, survival-oriented, pragmatic, suspicious, streetwise, work-to-live (as opposed to live-to-work), realistic, having a get-along attitude, community oriented, and not optimistic about their future in a changing world.

Unlike the Boomers who were brought up in a relatively secure and stable family environment, Generation X children grew up during an era when family life was breaking down. Boomers focused on pursuing the American economic dream at considerable expense to the children they brought into the world. Divorce rates increased dramatically in this era; "latchkey kids" became a new term in the American vocabulary; abortion was legitimized; and a high percentage of Xers grew up in homes without both birth parents. It was an era when children were devalued in general, were no longer the primary focus of parental concern, and were often required to face challenges previously reserved for adulthood, including household responsibilities like cooking, caring for siblings, shopping, etc. Some key characteristics follow:

- As children of divorce and dysfunctional families, many Xers face disruptive consequences. Studies reveal children of divorce often have little ambition and drift through life without goals and with a sense of helplessness.
- Divorce has made this generation less inclined toward early marriage. Later marriage and economic conditions cause many to return home after college until they can become self-sufficient.
- In terms of family values and marriage, Xers tend to put family and friends first and job second.
- They have adopted a survival or adaptive mentality and a simpler approach to life in an increasingly complex world. They anticipate a bleak economic future.
- In terms of trust, their survival mentality and the broken promises experienced during childhood tend to make them respond to deeds rather than words or symbols.
- Having learned to survive by avoiding conflict, they ignore or work around authority. Similarly, truth must be lived out, not stated.
- They are socially conscious, but not in the same sense as the radical social movements of the 1960s. They are not trying to change the world like their parents did, but are inclined toward a one-on-one outreach to fill a need or community issue.

- Beyond changing societal attitudes toward sex, increased sexual activity of Xers is thought to relate to the lack of intimacy at home and a poor self-image.
- They have little trust in the political process.
- The painful environment of their youth (the latchkey kids, divorced parents, and abused children generation) has led to a high suicide rate, drinking problems, and vulnerability to stress.
- Perhaps most significantly, they yearn for community and increasingly satisfy this need through a community of friends—a new type of family in which they can place their trust.

Long emphasizes that Generation Xers crave intimate community and that small groups that accommodate this need are the key to effective ministries. All small group ministries do not fill this bill. Newcomers thrown together in a small group to get acquainted or participate in a Bible study rarely develop into the type of community that Long feels is needed to minister to and hold the Xers. In order to evolve into the community that Xers desire and need, the small group needs deeper sharing that develops over time through activities beyond their meetings, such as meals, movies, shopping, or sporting events. Long states:[8]

> While boomers may stand anonymously on the fringes of a church, Xers want to become involved. While boomers have a hard time sharing with a group, Xers want to dialogue. The kinds of ministries that we have established for the boomer generation are not effective with the Xer generation. One example is the seeker service. Boomers, who are more self-assured and autonomous, want to be left alone to observe and decide for themselves when to get involved. Xers, as part of the emerging postmodern generation, need to be invited in because they are not self-assured. Once they are inside the door, they want to become part of the community, not remain aloof.
>
> While the seeker service may provide an initial introduction to the church or Christian fellowship, Xers need to be invited into a more intimate community almost immediately. Otherwise, they will drift away. We need to establish an effective method of drawing Xers into an intimate community as soon

as possible once they express an interest in our church or Christian fellowship.

George Barna in *Evangelism That Works* describes the methods that are likely to have the greatest influence on Generation X or the Baby Busters:[9]

1. Cell groups, provided they are discussion oriented, non-confrontational, and non-impositional
2. Social welfare ministry opportunities that utilize a soft sell
3. Lifestyle evangelism strategy
4. Socratic evangelism, a dialectic method that has been in vogue in past centuries but has fallen into disfavor in this country

Busters also appreciate instructional methods that do not require tacit acceptance and rote memorization of imposed principles and truth or how to gain it. That condition, they believe, differs from person to person and can only be identified through a personal discovery journey.

THE YOUTH

Youth represent about 10 percent of the population, and over half are the tail end of Generation X. Referring back to Exhibit 2.4, the resurgence in birth rate for the Youth generation has all the initial earmarks of another bubble in the making that is characteristic of the one that launched the Baby Boomers. It is clear that this new generation will become increasingly significant on the basis of sheer numbers as they move into adulthood. It is also vitally important for the church to influence churched youth while it still has the opportunity. These statistics highlight the importance of ministries that reach unchurched youth while they are in this intellectually inquisitive phase of life and still open to new ideas. As to ministry emphasis, much of what has been said about Generation X also applies to the Youth category. Some of the key characteristics of today's teenagers according to a nationwide survey among a random sample of 732 youth, ranging in age from thirteen to eighteen, include the following:[10]

- They have a spiritual hunger and are receptive to discussions about truth, meaning, purpose, life and death, and God.
- Their learning process is oriented toward discussions, not lectures, implying a different teaching approach from that of earlier generations. They want to draw their own conclusions and will not accept beliefs being imposed upon them based in traditional values. They are skeptics.
- They are under a high stress level. These stresses include school, family, peer pressure, sexuality, crime threat, political correctness, and other tensions that are collectively much greater than those experienced by earlier generations.
- They tend to be self-reliant. This self-reliance arises out of necessity in some cases as parents are either unable or do not have the time to help. In other cases this reflects a greater degree of understanding on issues than has been historically true for this age group.
- They are less oriented than the Boomers toward long-term goals, materialism, idealism to change the world, and goal-setting for career growth, and more oriented toward survival, emotional wholeness, personal relationships, and development of their own families.
- Their concept of absolute truth is vague and rejected by most. In their reality truth is relative to the individual and the situation. Four out of five reject absolute moral truth.
- About one-third are being raised in households in which only one natural parent is present and where most divorced moms who remarry get divorced a second time. This has had a devastating impact on teens in terms of depression, a sense of loneliness and rejection, self-esteem, anger, guilt, and lack of achievement.
- They have adopted the new perception of family as individuals who deeply care for one another, a potentially fluid and transitory aggregation that leads to cohabitation, promiscuous sexuality, and single parenthood.
- The behavior of teenagers classified as Christians did not differ in many ways from that of non-Christian teenagers. Christian teenagers did hold a more traditional view of marriage, were more interested in having a close relationship with God, and had a clearer purpose for living. They were also more like-

ly to believe in the Bible and absolute truth. But an evaluation of lifestyles, attitudes, and beliefs of Christian teens in comparison to Biblical standards correlated poorly. However, a close parallel between Christian teens and Christian adults in this regard indicates errant doctrine on the part of adults who influence the teenagers.

The primary implications to ministry are not so much an issue of programming as one of approaches taken by youth leaders. Barna emphasizes that teenagers want help, acceptance, love, and truth, not sermons, lectures, and games. They need to be befriended, encouraged, and introduced to Christianity through practical Bible lessons and principles that they can immediately apply in their lives. They also need help with real life problems such as homework, resolving conflicts, job hunts, and similar needs. If the church is to have an impact on this age group, Barna emphasizes that the church must demonstrate in a practical way that the family of Christ integrates faith into all aspects of life. He states:[11]

> The most effective means of influence is to adopt a firm but interactive style. Teenagers, especially in the late '90s, resent and resist imposed standards. They are often not opposed to standards as much as they are resentful of how those standards were presented and instituted. The influencers who make the biggest dent in the thinking and lifestyles of teens are those who enable them to understand and own the parameters they need. Discussing the problems, potential solutions and preventative courses of action can enable teens to believe they can have a stake in both the proceedings and the outcomes. It is that sense of participation that makes the standards more palatable and more likely to be implemented.
>
> But leaders who are not accessible to teens are unlikely to have much influence on them. Credibility comes from involvement; involvement requires availability.

THE PRE-BOOMERS

The Pre-Boomers encompass the Builders (born 1927-1945) and the Blazers (born before 1927). In 2000, the Builders fall into the age category of fifty-five to seventy-three and the Blazers seventy-four and older. They are typically described as faithful, loyal, trusting in leadership, stable, cautious, conservers, and oriented toward delayed gratification (rather than the instant gratification of Boomers). Pre-Boomers represent about a quarter of the population and will be the fastest growing population segment as the Boomers age into this bracket. Social observers predict issues on aging and the elderly will become dominant in 2011, as the first Boomers enter their sixty-fifth year. By the year 2025, Americans over sixty-five will outnumber teenagers by more than 2 to 1, and by the year 2050, one-fifth of all Americans will be over age sixty-five.[12]

Although the future lies with the younger generations, it is important to recognize that Pre-Boomers still represent a significant part of the church's market. Beyond the reality of sheer numbers, their discretionary income is high and they are stable and loyal churchgoers who have formed the habit of consistent giving. Since their children have grown and they are either approaching or are in retirement, they have more time for volunteerism. Perhaps most important, they represent a large talent pool that goes largely untapped or underutilized. Although Pre-Boomers seek less commitment so that they can have the freedom to travel and enjoy life, and although they are ready to turn over the reins of leadership to those younger, they nevertheless represent an important resource and are a stabilizing influence as the younger generations seek to "find themselves."

An article in the September 2, 1999, issue of *The New York Times* reports that a survey by Peter D. Hart Research Associates confirmed the fact that older Americans are generally overlooked or ignored as a valuable resource. Its poll of 803 men and women ages fifty to seventy-five found that older adults have a difficult time finding meaningful volunteer opportunities and that they feel that their skills are not valued by organizations. "People are tired of stuffing envelopes," the sponsor of the poll noted, adding that his own grandmother, a retired clothing store manager, was frustrated by the only volunteer job she could find, pushing a gift cart in a Philadelphia hospital.[13]

Pre-Boomers are largely oriented to the traditional programming that most churches are trying to transition away from as they seek to appeal to the younger generations. Accordingly, a lot of new innovative programming is not necessary to accommodate this group. They may tolerate, but do not embrace, the contemporary music and worship format changes that are taking place. For that reason, more and more churches are making a transition to two worship services—one traditional and the other contemporary.

The ministry implication is the need for balance as churches increasingly transition to accommodate younger generations. The tendency of herding Pre-Boomers into groups that are comprised exclusively of seniors is resented by some that regard this as segregating them from the mainstream into senior holding pens. Moreover, the tendency to "shelve" seniors helps to produce a self-fulfilling prophecy. They are being given the message that they are no longer important and, consequently, many accept this and withdraw from active involvement. One solution worth considering is to provide at least one Sunday school class that is intergenerational in membership. This is also true for some of the small group ministries. Although preceding discussion suggests that the primary focus of many small group ministries is to accommodate relational and support needs of Boomers and Xers, some intergenerational home fellowships and/or Bible study groups may not only be appropriate but extremely beneficial.

The First Baptist Church of Lake Hills, Bellevue, Washington, addressed this issue. In a recent conversation, the pastor described his church's "flock ministry." Small groups of thirty to forty people meet once a month either in homes or at the church. They have a light meal and good fellowship together, share needs and experiences, enjoy a sense of mutual support and care, and have the opportunity to build friendships and relationships. It is also a good way to integrate newcomers into the church fellowship and to provide a friendly environment where unchurched friends can be invited and feel comfortable. The pastor stressed that these flock groups were, by design, intergenerational in makeup. He believed this was important because it provided the opportunity for younger members to observe the rich heritage reflected in the lives of older members in terms of stable family relationships, long-standing and fulfilled marriages, and unconditional commitment to each other in the marriage relationship. He explained that these values may never have been experienced by younger people in his congregation, many of whom are the product of divorced parents, blended families, or dysfunctional family situations. The emphasis today on age grouping is believed to be overdone and seems to reflect a mind-set that carries over from the educational experience (public and Sunday school class groupings) where it has a valid purpose.

The flock ministry previously described, incidentally, is just a part of a twelve-month strategic plan that the church puts into effect annually. This plan encompasses a carefully structured schedule of events that is designed to attract and assimilate unchurched people into church involvement through a gradual and nonthreatening process. It reflects a proactive shift today among progressive churches toward the development of strategic plans designed to translate purposes and goals into realities.

In today's environment there are many other areas where Pre-Boomers can be productively used. This is a win/win situation that fulfills the need among Pre-Boomers to still feel relevant while also enhancing the ministries of the church. For example, the large number of dysfunctional and single parent families in today's society presents many such opportunities. Areas of service might include Big Brother or Big Sister ministries; child care, shopping breaks, and other assistance to single parents; or children and youth ministries that can benefit from the experience and role model influence that seniors can provide. Pre-Boomers are also important in mentoring new leadership and providing an intergenerational balance in leadership roles. Their involvement can add experience, stability, and continuity to temper the more aggressive and risk-oriented posture of younger leaders.

> After all, the Earl of Halsburg was 90 when he began preparing his 20-volume revision of English law. Galileo made his greatest discovery at age 73. Hudson Taylor was laboring vigorously on the mission field at age 69. Goethe wrote Faust at 82. And at the age of 85 Caleb wanted a mountain so that he could drive out a stronghold of giants. (Joshua 14:10-15)[14]

An important and overlooked factor in ministering to Pre-Boomers is the growing number of singles emerging when one spouse dies. This is particularly true for widows since women live longer than men on average. The problem is escalating as life expectancies increase and medical procedures extend life. Most church programs, regardless of intent, are designed for and cater to couples. Older singles often feel unwanted, uncomfortable, and somewhat excluded from these couples-oriented church events. Churches need to explore this problem and design ways to erase this bias in current programming, as well as launch new programs for singles. Actually, the problem of increasing numbers of singles is not restricted to the seniors, but applies to all age levels given present divorce levels and as more women are "liberated" in today's society. However, it is particularly difficult at the senior level when adaptation to "singles" status is much more difficult.

MINISTRY IMPLICATIONS

In the keynote address at the 1999 Annual Conference of Regular Baptist Churches, Dr. J. Don Jennings focused on the need for ministry change. His comments encapsulate to a large degree the essence of what those most prominent and in the forefront of future ministries planning have been telling us. Accordingly, the changes in approach that he advocates for a vibrant ministry in our times merit serious consideration. The following extract of his address provided in a booklet summarizes the ministries that he believes churches must develop to remain relevant:[15]

1. *Ministries that are Mission based rather than tradition based.* Each church should develop a mission statement. The mission statement is a definition of the key ministry objectives of the church. It is designed to unite people in ministry for the glory of God. The church should not be doing what it is doing just because it has always done that. Mission, not tradition, should drive the church.
2. *Ministries that promote participation, not observation.* The postmodern, electronics-focused generation learns differently from their print-oriented parents. We will need to provide a new learning environment and encourage and provide for interactive learning experiences.
3. *Ministries that are focused not exclusively on the individual but inclusively on the family unit.* "The future of the church in

America depends largely upon the spiritual commitment of families" (Barna). For the sake of the future of the church, we must integrate families into the mix of goals and activities of the church.
4. *Ministries that are built upon relationships not programs.* Christianity is more relational than organizational. People need better relationships, not better programs.
5. *Ministries that accentuate audience-based worship, not performance-based worship.* Sit-and-soak worship services create pew potatoes! Worship is not a spectator sport.
6. *Ministries that are designed to minister, not to entertain.* Let us stop calling entertainment "ministry." Our ministries must be authentic, credible, and spiritually enriching experiences.
7. *Ministries that are decentralized, not centralized.* Group studies, networking, and team ministries make for a strong ministry. For help in this area, read *The Synergy Church* by Michael C. Mack and published by Baker. This is a strategy for integrating small groups and Sunday school. The old adage, "Many hands spoil the pudding" may be true in the kitchen but it is not true in the church's ministry. The more involved the better!
8. *Ministries that empower horizontally instead of vertically.* Unless people are empowered to serve each other and the world they will only be serving the organization.
9. *Ministries with dual focus on evangelism and edification, not just one or the other.* If we are thoroughly biblical in our ministry, we will obey all of the Commission in Matt. 28 and both evangelize and stabilize with equal earnestness.
10. *Ministries that reproduce themselves regionally and cross-culturally by birthing new churches.* The church that does not start, or partnership with others to start, new churches is an organism without an offspring, a condition to be avoided at any expense!
11. *We need to get back to House Church Planting.* House churches offer convenience in scheduling and location, are highly relational, and do not require large outlays of money for buildings and overhead. They represent the ultimate in flexibility. A ministry that reproduces itself regionally should also do so cross-

culturally by sending its own members out to do Career and/or Tent-making or Short-term ministry.

Exhibit 2.5 provides another perspective of ministry implications in terms of the major generational groups.[16] The different perspectives of the three adult generational cultures make mutual understanding among each sometimes difficult. Each has grown up in a different world with a different set of values, experiences, and circumstances. One of the ways to alleviate this problem might be to offer some type of intergenerational education program or seminar that covers the differences in how the Pre-Boomers, Boomers, Generation Xers, and Youth each view the world, as well as one another, and why. Much of the material in this chapter and in the other sources referenced would provide the basis for developing such a curriculum. A workshop or Sunday school class would provide the appropriate forum. Such a program could go a long way to bring about a closer sense of unity and understanding between the different age levels. Understanding often leads to better acceptance and tolerance and could pave the way for possible changes that the church may want to implement following an evaluation using the Ministries Matrix process described in Chapters 6 and 7.

EXHIBIT 2.5. Ministry Implications

Ministry Aspect	Pre-Boomers	Boomers	Generation X
Scope of Ministries	• Adequate to sustain balance of traditional programs	• Full-service • Good children/ youth ministries/ facilities	• Strong emphasis on relational groups
Church Loyalty	• High • Institutional	• Low ⟶ • People-oriented	• Issues-oriented
Worship Format	• Hymns • Ceremonial • Minimal audience participation • Routine • Traditional music	• Praise songs/choruses ⟶ • Informal/celebration ⟶ • High audience participation • Variety ⟶ • Contemporary music ⟶	• Limited audience participation

Sermons	• Expository • Exhortive	• How-to	• Issues-oriented
Christian Education	• Sunday school —————————————————→		
		• Small groups ——————————————→	
Bible Study	• In-depth	• Practical • Life needs	• Issues-oriented
Evangelism	• Mass • General population • Revivalistic	• Support groups • Friendship ———— • Personal —————	• Relational ————————→ ————————→
Stewardship	• Total ministry • Program • Missions	• People-oriented • Special projects ———	• Community causes ————————→
Small Groups	• Fellowship • Bible study • Scheduled	• Support groups as needed • Scheduled	• Community • Relational • Involvement • Scheduled/unscheduled

Chapter 3

Priorities

The establishment of ministry priorities is a key element in the management process described in subsequent chapters. The relative priorities assigned to various ministry categories will be influenced by many factors. One is the market described in the preceding chapter. Most churches would view a strong ministry emphasis toward Generation X and Baby Boomers as a high priority because of the population size of these markets and their strategic significance in terms of outreach potential, as well as in carrying on the purposes and work of the church as the Pre-Boomers fade from the scene. The same might be said for the Youth generation as the growing birth bubble for this age level foretells their future significance. Another influence in setting priorities is the perceived relative importance of defined purposes as related to each age category or generational group. Still other influences might include church size and the characteristics and needs of the community. This chapter touches upon several of these influences that are viewed as particularly important, along with some related ministry ideas that churches have found to be effective.

CHILD EVANGELISM

Evangelism is most certainly a primary purpose of every evangelical church. Based on several studies, a case can be made that some age groups are strategically more important concerning evangelism than others. Child evangelism appears to be one of the most important but neglected areas of evangelism.

The following data is published by Child Evangelism Fellowship (CEF) and indicates when people become Christians.[1]

Age at Conversion	Percentage
Under 4 years old	1%
4-14 years old	85%
15-30 years old	10%
Over 30 years old	4%

Similar conclusions have been reported by George Barna in *Generation Next:*[2]

> For a large number of Americans, the key time of decision in life is in the 10- to 12-year age span. Although kids in this age range constitute only 4 percent of the population, it is the time frame when more than one-quarter of all believers decide to follow Jesus Christ.
>
> In fact, if we stretch the age frame to 8 to 13 years of age, that six-year stretch of time defines when roughly half of all Americans made their decisions to become Christians. In other words, by the time students enter high school, the odds of accepting Christ as Savior are radically reduced; by the time they graduate from high school the odds are stacked against such a choice to a staggering degree.

The view that children and youth are particularly receptive to the Christian message is further reinforced by the age distribution of those who respond to invitations at Billy Graham Crusades. According to statistics supplied by the Graham follow-up department, the percentage breakdown of 16,520 inquirers who came forward at a typical ten-day crusade was as follows:

Age Range	Percent of Inquirers
5-10 years	14%
11-15 years	24%
16-19 years	16%
20-25 years	12%
26-39 years	14%
40-49 years	7%
50 and over	8%
Undetermined	5%
	100%

Since Billy Graham Crusades are geared primarily toward adults, it is significant that 38 percent of those responding to the invitation were below sixteen years of age.

A tendency toward skepticism exists concerning whether very young children are capable of making a meaningful commitment of faith. Do children understand the significance of their actions in responding to an invitation to receive Christ as Savior, or are they responding in a way that they feel to be pleasing to the teacher or adult authority who offers the invitation? Statistics concerning the high conversion rate among children are sometimes discounted on the basis that adult Christians responding to such questionnaires have often been exposed to Christian instruction at a very young age through programs such as Sunday school, and erroneously refer to this early instruction, rather than to the age of actual conversion. However, even if this is true, it would be necessary to conclude that early Christian instruction has a profound spiritual impact on children, laying the groundwork for ultimate conversion for a high percentage of such individuals. Stated another way, even if it is assumed that children are incapable of a meaningful salvation decision, the statistics seem to indicate that very few individuals are converted to Christ unless they are exposed at a young age to Christian instruction.

Scripture supports the view that very young children can and do make meaningful and lasting decisions for Christ. J. I. Overholtzer, founder of Child Evangelism Fellowship, Inc., points out in "Child Evangelism As Taught in the Word of God"[3] that Christ responded to a question by the disciples concerning who should be the greatest in the kingdom by calling a little child and setting him in their midst (Matthew 18:1-14). The fact that he called the child suggests that this was not an infant (adults do not normally call infants and expect a response). The parallel scripture in Mark 9:36 reveals that he took the child in his arms, indicating that the child was indeed very young, probably not over eight years of age. His comments to the disciples in these verses would seem to be applicable to all such small children. In Matthew 18:3-4, Christ indicated that we must become as little children (as the one before them) in order to enter the kingdom of heaven, suggesting that the simple childlike faith and trust of a small child is necessary to come to faith in Christ, contrary to the view that children are incapable of exercising saving faith. Christ also indicated that whoever welcomes such a child in his name, welcomes Christ himself, emphasizing the importance of reaching small children (Matthew 18:5). Verse 14 states that it is ". . . *not the will of your Father which is in heaven, that one of these little ones should perish,*" (KJV) indicating that little children are spiritually capable of perishing as well as being the recipients of God's grace.

Child Evangelism Fellowship emphasizes that the validity of child evangelism is reinforced by practical experience, referring to the following.[4] Polycarp, the aged martyr of the early church, is reported to have become a believer at age nine; Matthew Henry at age ten; Isaac Watt at age nine; Jonathan Edwards at age seven; Count Zinzedorf, spiritual leader of the Moravians, at age four; Henrietta Mears at age five; Mrs. Billy Graham at age five; Corrie ten Boom at age five; evangelist Leighton Ford at age five; and psychologist and founder of Focus on the Family, Dr. James Dobson, at age three or four. A comprehensive study would undoubtedly extend this list of well-known Christians who date their conversion to a very early age.

Although statistics are important, the potential for reaching unchurched children with the Christian message was brought home in a more personal way by a close relative who is a nursing instructor residing in a large California city. Annoyed that the neighborhood children were making a practice of pestering her fifteen-year-old pet ducks, as well as getting into a variety of other forms of mischief, she decided the problem was rooted in the lack of constructive activities, and struck upon the thought of organizing a club. The kids were enthusiastic about the idea. They called it the "L and D" club, named after the intersecting streets, Lauderdale and Darwin, on which the home and meeting place was situated. It was to be a Bible club. A flannelgraph board and an array of visual aids were purchased from the local Christian supply center and a club was started. It turned out to be very similar in format and approach to the Child Evangelism Fellowship Good News Club program. The kids can hardly wait for club meeting days. They take care of the advertising and promotion themselves. Several large signs which read "L and D Club Meets Today" would appear at strategic locations throughout the neighborhood on meeting days. At their own initiative, the rough and tough little kids of this neighborhood decided that the letters "L and D" should have a deeper meaning and revised the official name to "Love and Discipline," a rather remarkable choice for this crew. These children are being presented the Gospel and are eager and receptive. They are also growing in Christ and in the Christian life. Several days after a "Good Samaritan" lesson, the woman who started this club returned home from work to notice three of the "gang" firmly planted on her garage driveway. The garage door had inadvertently been left open, an invitation to almost certain theft in this neighborhood. The three little "Good Samaritans" were there guarding things most of the day until she returned, and explained how this was their responsibility in taking care of one another, a lesson learned a few days earlier.

Examples like these help to remind us that the world's most fruitful mission field is probably right outside of our door—the unchurched children in our neighborhoods. Various surveys suggest that about 15 to 20 percent of the U.S. population can reasonably be classified as evangelical Christians. A more restrictive interpretation of the term "evangelical" would probably reduce this percentage. Assuming that about the same ratio of children are exposed to evangelical Bible teaching, it is apparent that the great majority of children receive no such exposure. There are over 35 million children between the ages of five and thirteen in the United States, and according to information compiled by Child Evangelism Fellowship ministries over the years, well over two-thirds of these are not attending any church at all. These statistics are particularly relevant when it is remembered that the great majority of Christian conversions occur during childhood.

This information emphasizes the tremendous evangelism opportunity concerning children who are currently outside of the direct influence of such traditional programs as the Sunday school. If unchurched children truly represent the promising evangelistic opportunity these statistics imply, then programs are needed that will reach children who are unable or unwilling to come to church. In other words, programs that will take the Gospel to the children where they are—in their own neighborhoods and environment. Christ did not instruct the world to go to the church, but He did tell the church to go into all the world and teach.

One solution to this program need is remarkably simple and can be implemented rapidly with dramatic results. It involves the establishment of weekday Bible clubs that meet in neighborhood homes. Unchurched parents are often quite willing to permit their children to attend Bible clubs held in neighborhood homes of people they know, even though they may be unwilling to have them attend church. In addition, the informal environment of the home and the fact that most of the children know one another beforehand, makes it very easy to enroll a large number of children very rapidly. Since the clubs meet each week, the children receive continued spiritual nourishment and follow-up on a weekly basis. Moreover, the teacher or hostess of the club, who also lives in the neighborhood, becomes a spiritual counselor who is always available to encourage and answer questions that arise from time to time.

The simplest way to get this type of program underway is through the assistance of Child Evangelism Fellowship (CEF), an international organization with local offices throughout the United States. Its major ministries are home Bible clubs, called Good News Clubs and Five-Day Clubs, although it also has a variety of other ministries as well. The Good News Clubs sponsored by CEF can be organized through individuals or through churches. In the latter case, CEF functions as a service organization in much the same manner as Christian Service Brigade or Pioneer Ministries. CEF conducts weekly teacher training classes and publishes a wide range of excellent teaching materials and visual aids that are available at a reasonable cost. Experience demonstrates that it is not unusual to have twenty clubs in operation within two months after a children's home Bible club program is initiated. Club attendance typically consists of ten to twenty children per club, equating to an outreach ranging from 200 to 400 children each week. Most of these children do not attend church or Sunday school.

Child evangelism has been endorsed by such evangelical notables as Harry A. Ironside, Charles G. Trumbull, Paul W. Rood, Walter L. Wilson, MD, and Henry C. Thiessen, all of whom were instrumental in the founding of Child Evangelism Fellowship through their support to the organization's founder, J. Irvin Overholtzer. The bottom line: do not overlook child evangelism as you prioritize your mission categories.

Another area that merits serious attention concerning priorities for children-oriented ministries is some type of counseling or other ministry that responds to the emotional needs of children of single-parent homes. It is estimated that one in every three school-age children in the United States lives in a single-parent home. Often these children have no idea that the feelings they are experiencing in response to the changes in their family are normal. They need a place to share how they feel, learn how to deal with their emotions appropriately, and experience God's love. A good example of a ministry that does this is the "Pieces to Peace" ministry of Overlake Christian Church in Redmond, Washington. This is an effective ministry that has been developed over several years for parents and children (ages four to twelve) who are living in single-parent homes. Although not a counseling program, this ministry does provide the opportunity for children to discuss their emotions and needs with understanding adults. It helps both parents and children to handle the emotions of guilt, separation, loss, denial, and anger the child feels when there is a death, divorce, separation, or abandonment in the family. These changes have a traumatic effect on all those involved, but particularly on children. The program holds separate sessions for parents and children over an eight-week period, using various activities (skits, puppets, etc.) to bring out issues to discuss. It provides a forum where these children can express their pain and feel loved. Churches can contact Overlake Christian Church to learn more about the program by calling them at 425-702-0303. Another good source of help in this regard is the "Confident Kids" curriculum available from Standard Publishing, 8121 Hamilton Avenue, Cincinnati, Ohio 45231 (1-800-543-1353).

Big Sister and Big Brother programs that are sponsored by the church also minister to children of single parents. These programs can do much to help fill the voids for such children in terms of meeting emotional needs, and providing adult role modeling and involvement in the life of a child. This involvement would normally occur under a two-parent family but is often missing in a single-parent situation.

YOUTH EVANGELISM

The CEF surveys cited earlier imply that the youth age group is also extremely important in terms of both evangelism and discipleship opportunities. As noted earlier, 85 percent of people who become Christians do so between the ages of four and fourteen. It is unfortunate that the data is not broken down into smaller age increments, but we can still draw certain conclusions concerning youth. Assuming the dividing line between children and youth to be age twelve, it is apparent that the 85 percent figure reflects a mixture of both children and youth. The statistics also imply that the primary opportunity for evangelizing youth exists with the younger members of this age bracket, since only 10 percent of Christians are converted in the next age bracket, ages fifteen through thirty. These conclusions are reinforced by George Barna's surveys[5] that indicate about three-quarters of all Christian conversions occur before the eighteenth birthday. His research reveals that more than 70 percent of moneys spent by evangelical churches on evangelism is directed toward adults even though such effort has proved to be relatively ineffective. In contrast, funds spent on evangelizing young people have paid off handsomely.

The teenage years are crucial in terms of the church's opportunity to not only evangelize but instill Christian values in youth. Many young people are in church largely at parental insistence. For others it is an exploratory phase in life to consider many ideas, including religion. Barna's survey indicates that only 41 percent said they are very likely to attend a church once they leave home. The time that they are in church, therefore, represents the window of opportunity to influence them in terms of faith, values, and lifestyle.

A study conducted some time ago by Roy B. Zuck and Gene A. Getz, "Christian Youth: An In-Depth Study,"[6] also provided interesting insights into spiritual issues concerning youth. Since the study is now about thirty years old, its findings are dated but still worth considering. It surveyed several thousand youth who attended a broad spectrum of evangelical churches. About 29 percent of the teenagers indicated that a parent was the most influential factor in their Christian conversion. The church, its personnel, and its programs were credited as being the most important factor by about

28 percent of the teens. Thirty-six percent said that programs or activities outside of the local church were the most influential factors in their conversion.

Several conclusions are possible from these findings. Although almost 90 percent of the youth came from homes where one or both parents were Christians, only a third of those parents were the primary reason for their teen's conversion. This indicates the need for parental help and training concerning the parenting role and spiritual responsibilities toward children (Deuteronomy 6:6-7; Ephesians 6:4; Proverbs 22:6). As noted, the church was the primary influence in the conversion of 28 percent of the youth, compared to 36 percent for influences apart from either the church or parents. This leads to the question of whether the church is falling short in terms of an adequate evangelism emphasis toward youth. Another finding of the study was that about 10 percent of the youth who attended evangelical churches were not Christians. Although a small minority of youth in the church, they represent an important segment. Unless they are won to Christ while still in church, studies confirm that a high percentage will drop out at an early age with the odds against future conversion.

The other obvious reason that youth and children ministries are so important is that they are among the primary concerns and considerations of their parents in selecting a church. Without excellent ministries to children and youth, neither parents, children, nor youth will be there.

How does the church respond to this strategically important age level? As emphasized in Chapter 2, the priority in terms of ministry seems to center more on leadership than programming. Those who lead the youth ministry today must understand the unique needs and differences of this generation from that of an earlier era. It requires leaders who are accessible, understand the interactive ministry style to which today's youth respond, and who are oriented toward becoming involved in helping them solve their real life problems. It follows that a priority in youth ministries is the selection and training of youth leaders to fill this bill. A full-time youth leader or minister of youth ought to be a high priority, even for smaller churches. Leadership training is also an important element. Just as corporations send key personnel to conferences and seminars to update them on the latest knowledge of how to do their job more effectively, churches need to do the same. Youth leaders need the benefit of all the insight they can get from others in the same role concerning ministry approaches and better understanding of youth in today's world. Youth leaders need to be periodically updated and motivated. The days of getting any well-intentioned, available layperson to handle youth work without a good understanding of today's youth culture and proper training in youth ministries are long since past.

Equally important in terms of training are programs that help parents to become better prepared for parenting youth in today's environment. As the Zuck and Getz study revealed, parental influence was not as high as one would expect in terms of important spiritual decisions made by their teenagers. That reality is probably even much more true today than when the Zuck and Getz study was done. The teen years usher in an abrupt change in which the compliant, enjoyable child, responsive to parental guidance and influence up to this point in life, suddenly metamorphoses into what can become a parent's worst nightmare. Most parents are unprepared for this, and by the time they finally learn by all kinds of mistakes, it is too late. Much good material is available on parenting teens from organizations such as Focus on the Family. These resources should be made available in a church library. Ideally, periodic classes should be taught by qualified instructors to provide the type of interactive discussion that would prove helpful to parents of preteens and teens.

ADULT EVANGELISM

Adults comprise about 75 percent of the U.S. population (age eighteen and above). The surveys mentioned earlier indicate that very few adults are converted to the Christian faith, probably less than 10 percent of all Christian conversions. The conclusion must be that adults are very difficult to evangelize, or the church has been ineffective in its outreach to them. Other surveys indicate that the latter may be more of a factor than generally realized. A Gallup survey[7] found that 96 percent of Americans say that they believe in God; 71 percent profess belief in an afterlife; 90 percent say they pray; and 41 percent say they attend religious services frequently. Surveys reported in *The Index of Leading Spiritual Indicators*[8] by George Barna indicate similar responses from adults: 87 percent of all adults state that their religious faith is very important to them; 74 percent said it would be very desirable to have a close relationship with God; 67 percent claim to have made a personal commitment of faith to Christ; 39 percent describe themselves as "born again," 18 percent as "evangelized," and 29 percent as "fundamentalist;" 85 percent consider themselves to be Christians; and almost 42 percent of adults attend church in a typical week.

These data present a paradox. How does a remarkably high rate of conservative Christian affirmations among adults translate into relatively low church attendance? Are these statistics of Christian affirmation meaningful or do they reflect use of the Christian "label" in the context of "Christian culturism," as opposed to true conversion? Or could they reflect erroneous self-perception in the context of misunderstanding or inadequate knowledge concerning biblically based truth? If all of the professing Christians of these surveys are true believers, we are either in a new paradigm in which most Christians no longer deem Christian assembly for worship and fellowship relevant—or the church is failing woefully to meet the need of believers. Beyond the incompatibility of conservative Christian profession versus practice reflected in the surveys, the reality of today's social attitudes argues that the statistics overstate the percentage of true believers. The deteriorating moral environment that prevails in all aspects of American life and the anti-Christian sentiment that is commonplace testifies to this viewpoint.

Whether the statistics reflect reality or not, however, they certainly put the church in a bad light. Even if they are valid and 85 percent of all adults are already Christians, it does not account for the low level of Christian conversions among adults. The American adult population comprises about 75 percent of the total. Even if only 15 percent of these are non-Christians, the non-Christian adult population would still exceed either the youth-aged population or the children-aged population, where the overwhelming number of Christian conversions occur. If the survey data overstates the percentage of true believers, it makes the adult conversion picture even more dismal.

Surveys show that about 85 percent of new converts are brought into the church by friends and relatives. Only 6 percent are brought in by an organized evangelism outreach, another 6 percent by the pastor, and 2 percent by advertisement.[9] Seventy percent, according to George Gallup, believe most churches and synagogues are not effective in helping people find meaning in life.[10] These data raise the possibility that evangelizing adults may not be quite the dry hole implied earlier—and indicates the need for a change in methods. Good preaching and strong traditional in-house ministries obviously are not enough. Today's conventional wisdom is that the church needs to reach out and minister to the unchurched where they are and establish some type of a connection as a prelude to inviting them into the church. Once in the church, polls reveal that the needs that newcomers are seeking to have fulfilled are:[11]

1. To believe life is meaningful and has a purpose
2. To have a sense of community and deeper relationships
3. To be appreciated and respected
4. To be listened to—and heard
5. To feel that one is growing in the faith
6. To have practical help in developing a mature faith

One weak link in adult evangelism may be a breakdown in adult discipleship ministries. Evangelism is the key to perpetuating and growing the church, but discipleship is the key to ensuring that evangelism takes place. The measure of how effective the church is in making disciples, therefore, is the effectiveness of its evangelism outreach.

Bill Hull in *7 Steps To Transform Your Church*[12] provides insight on this. He reports on information from data compiled by the Institute for Church Development, a church consulting and assessment ministry associated with Denver Seminary (800-359-5480, Gary Bateman, Director). Data compiled in a survey[13] involving over 500 churches and 130,000 church members in forty denominations revealed that an average of only 1.7 people were led to Christ per 100 people in attendance. In other words, an average evangelical church of 200 would typically win only 3.4 converts to Christ in a year. Hull also explains some of the reasons that more evangelism is not taking place, drawing upon findings from a survey by *Chris-*

tianity Today.[14] One reason is that people have a misconception of what evangelism is. So-called "friendship evangelism," for example, is mostly friendship and relationship building but not much evangelism that includes leading the person to Christ. Another reason is that many Christians do not believe every Christian needs to witness. It is Hull's experience that 25 percent of Baby Boomer evangelicals do not feel they are expected to verbalize their faith or seek to evangelize others. The *Christianity Today* survey found that the reasons given by respondents for their failure to evangelize are: fear; the moral failures of prominent electronic church (TV) Christian personalities, and the resultant ridicule and skepticism concerning the Christian faith; lack of time; and lack of confidence. Most of these reasons are a reflection on ineffective disciple making or training. It is also a matter of motivation and focus. Hull reports the results of a Baylor University survey of more than 1,100 churches:[15]

> Churches older than 20 years have an annual rate of conversion that is one-third that of churches under two years of age and 10 percent less than churches 10 to 20 years of age. There are at least two reasons for this. A church initially reaches out to gather enough people to support a pastor and have a church. Once this is achieved, its energy reverses from outward to inward. Church personnel are gobbled up by traditional church programs. The focus becomes institutional. The older a church gets, the more it becomes dedicated to survival for the sake of itself. This trend is creating the kind of deplorable evangelistic death that now characterizes more than half of our evangelical churches.

The survey also found that in older churches the pastor's focus is no longer outward but preoccupied with serving the members. The retention of new people is 20 percent less in older churches than in those only two to five years old. Older churches apparently lose their zeal in welcoming and integrating newcomers into the fellowship. This all suggests the need for better discipleship training. In most churches this is supposed to occur in the Sunday school and in home Bible studies. But in most evangelical churches the emphasis in these programs is educational and involves very little training.

Ken Hemphill and R. Wayne Jones in *Growing an Evangelistic Sunday School*[16] make a strong case for reorienting the Sunday school from an educational emphasis back to more of the evangelistic emphasis that once prevailed in evangelical churches. They report on the view of those who see the subtle shift away from evangelism to education in the Sunday school as a major contributing factor in the decline of their denomination and link it to liberal theology. The authors make the point that the Sunday school role should include reaching people for Christ, teaching the Bible, leading members to witness, leading members to minister, leading members to worship, and interpreting the work of the church and denomination. Of these, witnessing is described as the most critical and at the very heart of the Sunday school, not just a byproduct. Their book describes a Sunday school concept that is structured around evangelism in terms of organization, leadership training, visitation, worker meetings, and all other aspects of the program.

From the standpoint of using the ministries management system and Ministries Matrix described in later chapters in evaluating current programs, the importance of defining purposes of the church in specific terms becomes clear from the preceding discussion. For example, without a clear definition of discipleship as a purpose, the initial presumption might be that the existence of Sunday school and home Bible study programs means that the discipleship purpose is adequately covered. However, if discipleship is defined as including training that leads to effective evangelism, then the absence of such outcome would require reexamining the effectiveness and adequacy of such existing discipleship-oriented programs. As described later, the implication from an action standpoint would be that either the current programs need to be reoriented to include a greater emphasis in training and motivating members to exercise their faith through personal witnessing, or that other new programs are needed to fill this apparent void.

CHURCH SIZE

Estimates as to the number of churches in America vary according to source. But the number is believed to be between 340,000 and 500,000, depending upon how "church" is defined. This includes

Roman Catholic, Mormon, Jewish synagogues, Orthodox Church congregations, and Jehovah's Witnesses, which together represent about 40,000 of the total. Most of these churches are small. Surveys indicate that about half have an attendance of seventy-five or less at morning worship, less than 2 percent are megachurches (2,000 or more) and only 17 to 20 percent have attendance of 200 or more on a weekend.[17] A Barna survey indicates that about half have congregations of less than 100; 25 percent have congregations of 200 to 400; and 3 percent have attendance of over 1,000 on weekends. Surveys also indicate there has been little or no real growth in church membership in recent years.[18]

These statistics indicate that most churches in America are small and that the trend toward large full-service churches is mostly at the expense of small churches, through a reapportionment of attendees. Gallup surveys confirm this and reveal that 85 percent of church membership growth is made up of people who church hop.[19] The increase in some denominations is largely offset by decrease in others.

What are the implications of these trends to church purposes and ministry priorities, particularly concerning small churches? As mentioned earlier, Boomers are drawn to and expect the variety and benefits of full-service churches, putting small churches at a disadvantage. That leaves Youth, the Pre-Boomers, and Generation X, as well as Children, as the primary markets open to small churches. Churches that focus solely on Pre-Boomers are destined to extinction. That means small churches, if they expect to grow, must also focus upon the Youth and Xers. As they grow, they can also expand their ministry emphasis to include Boomers. As already mentioned, Generation Xers seek the intimate community of small group ministries. The small church congregation in toto may embody this characteristic to a substantial degree, particularly in new start-up churches that have been born with the vision to reach this hurting generation and are led by pastors and leadership that understand them. It is much more difficult for this to happen in small churches steeped in the traditions important to Pre-Boomers, namely older churches that have been in existence for some time. However, unless such a transition is made, most of these churches will likely struggle along for quite awhile at status quo level but eventually phase out as attendance declines with the aging of Pre-Boomers, and the shift continues to larger churches until the congregation becomes too small to be sustained. New small churches will continue to spring up as they are today, but which have the vision and agenda to minister to Generation X and those that follow.

However, all older small churches are not preordained to extinction. Some will survive, at least for a time, to accommodate Pre-Boomers and those among younger generations that remain traditional-ministry oriented, rather than conforming to the general mold of their peers. It is possible for others to make the transition, minister to Generation X, as well as older generations, and not only survive but grow. But it will not happen easily or automatically and probably a pastor will be needed who understands Xers and today's youth, has the passion to reach them, and the ability to impart this vision to both the church leadership and his congregation. An educational process will be required so that older generations operating on an entirely different cultural wavelength can acquire a better understanding of this outreach opportunity that focuses on youth and Xers. Changes required will include the formation of small group ministries and format changes of the type touched upon in Chapter 2.

Second, an effective evangelism outreach, important in the vision of all evangelical churches, is particularly critical for the small church as it seeks to achieve real growth. Real growth refers to attracting nonchurchgoers into the church. The other type of growth, attracting churchgoers from other churches, is not a plausible strategy for small or large churches. It is a zero-sum game that contributes nothing in terms of adding to the body of Christ. It is simply a reapportionment of believers, usually from smaller to larger churches. Without real growth, even churches that prevail in the competition for believers would eventually cease to exist. Unlike small churches, large churches have the resources and appeal to focus on all age categories or generational groups. Priorities for large churches are therefore influenced by issues other than the inherent size-related constraints described above.

COMMUNITY SERVICE OR ASSISTANCE

Attracting the unchurched into the church is one of the major problems facing churches today. The problem seems to be worsening. George Barna surveys indicate that the unchurched population has been rising.[20] Surveys indicate that the most important factors in attracting individuals to church involve help in problem solving and in meeting pressing needs. Primary needs identified were financial, employment status, personal health, and family matters. Spiritual issues were low on the list. Churches generally do not convey concern on this broad spectrum of issues to the people they seek to attract. The surveys also indicate that churches have been successful in attracting the unchurched through nonreligious events such as sports leagues, social events, seminars, concerts, and community assistance. Those who attend these events or programs, or who are assisted in some way, are invited to attend the church's services. Another primary strategy to attract potential members is for churched people to develop close personal relationships with unchurched friends and then invite them to church.

Concerning the community service approach, I was privileged to write a biweekly *Community Impact Bulletin* for the Washington Family Council of Bellevue, Washington, for several years. One of the purposes of the bulletin has been to provide current information on legislative issues that have moral or family value implications. The goal is to help keep the state's Christians informed so that they can be better citizens. Another purpose of the bulletin is to provide ideas and programs to help strengthen families, encourage community outreach, and to communicate the efforts of churches throughout the state and beyond as a means of Christian outreach. Some of these programs have been reprinted in the following sections by permission of the Washington Family Council[21] and its president, Jeff Kemp, a former NFL quarterback who is doing a great job in this ministry. These are practical ways that churches can reach out to the unchurched to help meet real-life needs that surveys have indicated are vitally important.

Help for Single Moms

Belmont Church of Nashville, Tennessee, conducts a widows' ministry that reaches out to single moms and widows in the neighborhood. It provides needed assistance with car maintenance and training and financial management. One of the ministries is *Car Care Saturday*. A member who operates a garage makes his facility available to the ministry once every quarter. Other volunteers change oil, do safety checks, and other routine maintenance at no charge. The ministry is funded by a special offering, which is collected every fifth Sunday. Single parents who participate also receive a copy of Larry Burkett's book, *The Complete Financial Guide for Single Parents*.[22] Other outreaches include *Seven Baskets*, a food and clothing program for low-income people. A *Big Buddy* program is planned to provide companionship for fatherless boys. The church also hopes to gather a team of men to do home improvement projects.

Special Delivery

Overlake Christian Church of Redmond, Washington, has purchased and remodeled a large two-story house for a ministry called *Special Delivery*. *Special Delivery* is a ministry committed to meeting the physical, emotional, and spiritual needs of pregnant unwed women and unwed mothers, providing an alternative to abortion. The broad-based ministry provides housing, counseling, birth classes, adoption assistance, a pre- and postparenting ministry, a storehouse program to provide clothing, food, and furniture for mothers and babies in need, and many other activities to help and provide for these women through their pregnancy and after, until they can handle life on their own.

World Relief Programs Offer Support to Refugee Families

World Relief has formed two programs designed to help refugee and immigrant families. One program, the Good Samaritan Network, helps families resettle in the United States; the other, a citizenship ministry, assists people seeking U.S. citizenship. World Relief reports that there are currently 17 million refugees in the world, more than ever before. In Washington State, World Relief needs volunteer churches that will provide classroom space, volunteers to act as instructional aides for the World Relief instructor, and people to befriend students and invite them to church and community events. Volunteers do not need intensive training, just a genuine desire to reach out to someone in need. For more information about these programs, contact World Relief at (206) 587-0234.

Church Teams Up with Pizza Shop to Improve Neighborhood

City Foursquare Church in the Queen Anne section of Seattle recently teamed up with Pagliacci Pizza by turning a closed hotel into a transitional housing complex for homeless men. As part of a drug abatement ordinance, the former Civic Center Motel was shut down after neighbors complained about prostitution, drug trafficking, and assaults. When Pagliacci Pizza bought the old motel, it leased out eight units in the back of the motel to the church at a generous price so the church could develop housing for up to twenty homeless men. In return for a place to stay at Valley Street House, as it is now called, the men will be required to attend church and work to support the operating fund for the house. The men receive job training and legal advocacy while at the home. Reverend Doug Heck, senior pastor of City Foursquare Church, wrote a letter to the neighbors asking them to donate money, labor, or materials to help renovate the housing units.

Helping Those in Need

Woodside New Life Assembly of God, Marysville, Washington, maintains a small building in downtown Marysville where each Tuesday a free meal is provided and clothing is available for those in need. Each third Saturday the building is opened for free haircuts, car repair, a meal, and clothing. In August, the outreach donates back-to-school items to students in need. The program is advertised on the radio and is run by various members of the congregation. The purpose of The Lighthouse is to meet the practical needs of the community and to earn the right to be heard.

Medical Care Ministry

Allegheny Center Alliance Church, Pittsburgh, Pennsylvania, together with three young physicians, has formed a health clinic to serve inner-city residents. The aim is to meet the physical, as well as the spiritual, emotional, and intellectual needs of inner-city residents.

Remedial Reading Program

According to Dr. Tim LaHaye, President of Family Life Seminars, students are failing because of the inept reading system and the lack of public discipline in public schools—not because they cannot learn. This represents a golden opportunity for churches/synagogues to reach out to the community. How? Find teachers within the congregation to use the excellent phonics-based programs available to teach remedial reading to neighborhood children after school. Teachers could also assign Bible-based reading to their students in much the same way that missionaries in many countries teach English. The church could well become the most respected institution in the community under such a program.

Dresser Ministry

Ann McNitt, in her desire to do something to help needy pregnant women in her community, had an inspiration. She would invite her church, Plymouth Brethren of DeWitt, Michigan, to fill a dresser with baby items and donate the entire unit to a local pregnant woman. Among the items solicited for donation were diapers and other diaper paraphernalia, baby bottles, blankets, clothing, shampoo, children's Tylenol, a thermometer, socks, T-shirts, pacifiers, a children's Bible, and a first aid kit. The dresser was taken to a crisis pregnancy center and given to a college student who had intended to abort, but changed her mind. McNitt was told that the dresser had really encouraged the student. This led to the designing of a complete kit instructing others on how to put together one of these dressers. *Focus on the Family* magazine described the idea in a 1993 issue, resulting in 1,700 of these instruction kits being sent to families in all fifty states and several foreign countries. One church in McNitt's hometown has filled twenty-one dressers. This project would be a great ministry outreach for a Sunday school class, a youth group, or a family. To receive a kit, write Ann McNitt, 6330 Herbison Road, DeWitt, MI 48820.

Parenting Workshops

Parenting workshops, patterned after those started six years ago in the greater Tacoma area under *Youth for Christ* sponsorship, are now being conducted in Seattle's Rainier Valley. *Emerald City Outreach Ministries* and *Union Gospel Mission* are cosponsoring the Rainier Valley workshops. These six-week programs are free and are conducted in cooperation with local churches, as well as with schools or community centers, which provide the facilities, advertising, and publicity. Each weekly session (of about two hours) starts off with a hot meal served by the host church, followed successively by instructional and small group discussion sessions led by church or sponsoring organization leaders. The children have their own age-oriented classes that include family-friendly videos, crafts, games, and talks about important issues. These "hands-on" outreach programs build relationships and meet needs in the community.

Community for Foster Care Program

On the grounds of a shuttered Air Force base in Rantoul, Illinois, an old-fashioned neighborhood has been created from scratch, right down to the stay-at-home moms and checkers-playing grandparents. And for the first time in his six-year-old life, Marc, a foster child who has cerebral palsy and a history of rejection, belongs to a family that wants him forever. "Are you going to be my daddy?" he asked Mark Owen, thirty-seven, his new foster father, a tall, broad-shouldered man in a work shirt. "I've never had a dad before." The answer came as a hug so tight and long it seemed that Mr. Owen would never let go.

In a pioneering two-year-old program for foster children who stand little chance of being placed in a family permanently, a University of Illinois professor of child development has drawn upon small-town closeness and nurturing she remembered from her childhood. After securing the purchase of sixty-three duplex apartments on twenty-two acres, the group, *Hope for the Children,* recruited and hired foster parents, who live rent free. The program pays one parent $18,000 a year to stay home with the children. The group also recruited middle-aged and elderly people who serve as "honorary grandparents." They receive subsidized rents in exchange for volunteering eight to ten hours a week as crossing guards, craft instructors, and maintenance workers. But their principal value comes in simply being part of the lives of the children, playing ball, lending an ear, and telling tall tales about the old days. The per-child costs at *Hope* average about $15,000 a year, compared to $60,000 plus (per child/per year) that the state pays for group homes for children who are difficult to place. Struck by the possibilities, officials of several states have made contact with *Hope for the Children,* with interest in developing similar programs. A major corporation is reportedly scouting the program and is considering financing a big expansion of it around the country. (Editor's note: Although too large an undertaking for a single church, this would seem a possibility for a denomination or group of like-minded churches.)

Community Renewal

A group of African-American pastors, together with the Northwest Leadership Foundation, have formed the Coalition for Community Renewal (CCR). As a first project they have purchased one home as a rehab and will build three new homes, providing four low-income families with affordable housing. Their vision for the future includes three acres in the heart of Rainier Valley (Seattle) where twenty-three homes would be built.

Multi-Faceted Community Impact Committee Approach

The Family Issues Committee of the Wenatchee Free Methodist Church in Wenatchee, Washington, has carried out the following programs during recent years:

- Maintains an information table and bulletin board in the foyer.
- Promoted the *Life Chain.* This is an annual event in which demonstrators line the main streets of many cities carrying signs that protest abortion.
- Maintains voter registration material on the information table and conducts *Voter Registration Sundays.*
- Sponsored a 4th of July program at the church.
- Sponsors a *Voter Forum* Sunday evenings prior to elections. The state *Voter's Guide* is reviewed with a panel of local legislators, and comments and questions are received from the audience.
- Provides bulletin inserts and announcements on legislative updates, and provides input on political issues to the church's weekly newsletter.

- Suggests special speakers and provides bulletin inserts for *Human Life Sunday.*
- Provides subscriptions to *American Family Association* magazine.
- Maintains pro-family magazines and videos in the church library.
- Works with the community *National Day of Prayer Mayor's Breakfast Committee.*
- Sponsored a church presentation on *Moms-in-Touch* to help launch the program.
- Sent cards to public school teachers regarding how to legally present the Christmas message in the public school setting.
- Prepared a *What Can I Do?* political action agenda.
- Provides initiative petitions on issues involving legislation designed to have positive pro-family implications. (Washington state provides for an initiative process whereby citizens can have an issue placed on the ballot by obtaining a specified number of signatures on an initiative petition.)

Church Promotes Spiritual, Economic Responsibility

A church in which 96 percent of the members once were on welfare and food stamps has become a model of economic success and spiritual hope. In 1977, the 200 members of Christ Temple Church in Meridian, Mississippi, took stock of themselves and their impoverished situation. Many had a long history of running up credit at the general store and faced a future of owing more than they made. The congregation pooled their resources and bought peanuts in fifty-pound sacks, repackaged, and resold them on the streets and in the stockyards. In four months, the church had enough money to make a down payment on a supermarket. Eventually, the church formed a nonprofit organization and added several other enterprises over the years. Members of the church work in the businesses. Today, no one in the congregation receives welfare or food stamps and everyone is employed.

Helping Single Parents

Single parent families in America now represent almost one-third of all families that have children. About one-fourth of all children now live with single mothers. About half of all children being raised by single mothers live below the poverty line. Senator Daniel Patrick Moynihan of New York writes that although poverty has historically come as a result of unemployment and low wages, today it derives from family structure. The underlying long-term solution obviously lies in reestablishing the two-parent family structure and reducing the illegitimacy and divorce rates in America. Until such time, however, a substantial number of single moms and their children face a daily crisis . . . financially, emotionally, and physically. The urgent opportunity exists for local churches to meet this challenge through *single moms* ministries. Following are some ideas concerning programs that might be considered by your church in this regard:

- Financial counseling (working, single mothers often face critical financial stress).
- Big Brother-type program (a significant number of children who live in fatherless homes see their fathers less than once a year).
- Auto maintenance assistance (volunteers perform routine auto maintenance on preset dates).
- Baby-sitting assistance (volunteers perform free baby-sitting service on occasion to allow financially limited moms to get out, run errands, and enjoy an occasional break).
- Home maintenance assistance (volunteers available to do simple home repairs).
- Formation of a single-parent support group (emotional support).

Community Involvement in Public Affairs

Tony Campolo, well-known author, evangelist, and professor at Eastern College (St. David's, Pennsylvania), suggests the need for local churches to regularly call meetings for all people (not just church members) in their communities, in a town-hall meeting format, to address local community problems. As an example, he cites his home church, which is located in a community made up largely of African Americans. When threats were made against an Asian family that owned a corner grocery store, the church leaders called the people of the community together to talk about what should be done. Although tense exchanges occurred, a clear course of action was agreed upon. The result was a public apology from the leaders of the African-American community to the frightened Asian family and a promise of the good citizens of the neighborhood to watch over the besieged store. Campolo encourages the church to do its thing on the local level to bring people together to make God's will known in their public affairs. A world suffering and groaning in travail (Romans 8:22) is hungry for it.

Public Stand on Pro-Family Issues

The Community Impact Committee of Richland Baptist Church in Richland, Washington, is involved in the following activities:

- Supports Tri-City Pregnancy Center.
- Promoted the *Life Chain* and *Walk for Jesus* events.
- Encourages community prayer by regularly praying for national, state, and local leaders and educators.
- Promotes Washington Consultation for United Prayer (W-CUP) events.
- Encouraging participation in the distribution of a petition to stop the showing of R-rated videos in our education system.

Chapter 4

A Word About Management

The focus of this chapter and those that follow turns to the subject of ministries management and a description of a ministries management process. Exhibit 4.1 provides a general overview, outlining the key elements in this process. It starts with defining the purposes for which the church exists (Step 1). This is translated into prioritized basic "mission categories," which adds the age and cultural orientation dimension to purposes and defines the areas for which responsive programs are needed. Next, an inventory is taken of current programming by mission categories to determine compatibility with defined purposes (Step 2). The intent is to identify programming imbalances, voids, or other inadequacies that need to be addressed. Step 3 is the formulation of revised program objectives as necessary. This may mean dropping some existing programs, initiating new ones, and/or redirecting others. Step 4 addresses the planned implementation process and the monitoring of progress.

Before getting into the specifics of this management process, some general observations are offered concerning the subject of management as applied in a church context. To "manage" simply means to contrive, to bring about, or succeed in accomplishing a predefined mission or objective. Management, the act or process of doing this, encompasses a broad spectrum of methods and techniques, including organization, planning, defining purpose, establishing objectives, monitoring progress, motivating, administering, and other similar functions. One of our evangelical shortcomings seems to be to regard management as acceptable insofar as the general administrative functions of the church are concerned, but with some suspicion when it comes to church ministries. This probably reflects concern that we may quench the Holy Spirit with regard to the

EXHIBIT 4.1

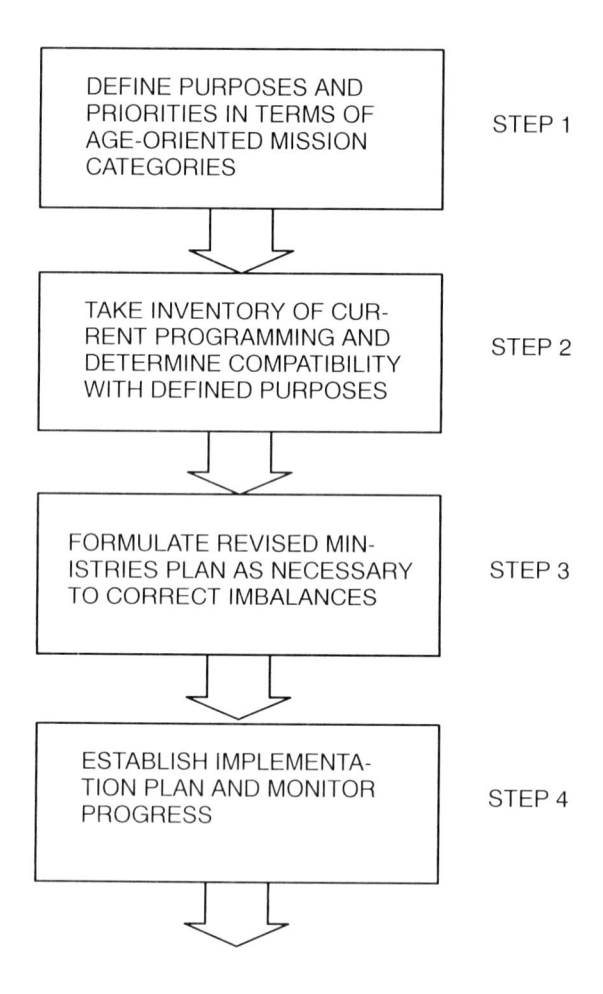

```
┌─────────────────────────────┐
│ DEFINE PURPOSES AND         │
│ PRIORITIES IN TERMS OF      │   STEP 1
│ AGE-ORIENTED MISSION        │
│ CATEGORIES                  │
└─────────────────────────────┘
              ↓
┌─────────────────────────────┐
│ TAKE INVENTORY OF CUR-      │
│ RENT PROGRAMMING AND        │   STEP 2
│ DETERMINE COMPATIBILITY     │
│ WITH DEFINED PURPOSES       │
└─────────────────────────────┘
              ↓
┌─────────────────────────────┐
│ FORMULATE REVISED MIN-      │
│ ISTRIES PLAN AS NECESSARY   │   STEP 3
│ TO CORRECT IMBALANCES       │
└─────────────────────────────┘
              ↓
┌─────────────────────────────┐
│ ESTABLISH IMPLEMENTA-       │
│ TION PLAN AND MONITOR       │   STEP 4
│ PROGRESS                    │
└─────────────────────────────┘
              ↓
```

spiritual ministries by substituting human wisdom and works for a faith-based dependency upon God. Some variation of the following question seems to surface from time to time: "Shouldn't we just pray and trust God for His blessings in these matters?" Management may be seen as a form of human manipulation that is fine for the secular world and routine administrative matters, but less appropriate for outreach ministries, reflecting the view that God's ecclesiastical system operates on a different plane.

The fallacy of logic that compartmentalizes church functions in this manner is readily apparent. Stewardship—tithing and giving—is a well-accepted scriptural and spiritual principle. But there is no direct scriptural reference to the accepted church functions associated with good stewardship—planning, budgeting, monitoring financial status, administering capital expenditures, structuring salaries and staffing, and the many other similar management practices.

Scripture provides basic principles and direction, but God apparently has avoided proclaiming hard and fast formulas, sacred techniques, or divine gimmicks for carrying on the work of the local church. Instead, He has left this to the individuality of His creatures and has made clear to men and women the power of the Holy Spirit to guide and direct their minds in fulfilling the church's mission. Scripture seems to confirm the appropriateness of good management principles in all aspects of local church work. Christ charged His disciples in Matthew 28:19-20 with the task of making and teaching disciples in all nations. But when He said, "Go therefore," He failed to specify the "how-to." Moreover, this charge appears to imply collective effort since believers were beginning to gather and meet in groups, which would ultimately evolve into local churches. The command to go to all nations, or to establish a foreign missions program, was certainly intended to convey collective effort, as well as individual responsibility. By its very nature, collective effort translates into the organization of effort, which requires direction and oversight—which is called "management." The implications of an organized collective effort in fulfilling the Great Commission, therefore, demonstrate the need for good management and methodology. But again, the specifics as to these were left to the discretion and wisdom of the apostles and the church, in general.

An example of God's endorsement of the management function is found in Exodus 18. Moses' father-in-law, Jethro, was used by God in a management consultant role to tell Moses to set up a management structure that would enable him to rule more effectively. In essence, Jethro advised Moses to reorganize and establish a structure of judges or regional authorities over the people to administer justice, rather than having the function carried out solely by

Moses. The fact that it was a well-organized structure with multiple tiers of management is evidenced by the fact that there were officers over groups of thousands, hundreds, fifties, and tens.

Acts 6 reveals that organization and management of time was a problem for the early Christians, just as it is for us today. This passage records the decision of the twelve apostles to delegate to seven appointed officials the work of "serving tables," or administering a food distribution program. Administration of the program had not been going well and there were complaints that the widows who spoke only Greek were being discriminated against, and were not being given as much food as those who spoke Hebrew. Perhaps more important, there was clear recognition that the apostles' objectives were not being accomplished in terms of the time and effort devoted to prayer and preaching. A new plan was therefore suggested that had never been done this way before, and yet the Bible indicates the entire congregation approved of this new management scheme. Verse 7 indicates the ensuing success of the change: "God's message was preached in ever widening circles, and the number of disciples increased vastly in Jerusalem; and many of the Jewish priests were converted too" (Acts 6:7 LB).

King Solomon provides a good illustration of effective management in the establishment of a highly efficient organization in which his realm was divided into twelve districts. That he was endowed with unique management skills is evidenced by his wealth, the flourishing commerce under his rule, his diplomatic successes, and the excellence of planning and supervision that must have prevailed in order to accomplish the monumental temple construction project. Note some of his God-inspired views that are recorded in Proverbs:

- The intelligent man is always open to new ideas. In fact, he looks for them. (Proverbs 18:15 LB)
- We should make plans—counting on God to direct us. (Proverbs 16:9 LB)
- Any enterprise is built by wise planning, becomes strong through common sense, and profits wonderfully by keeping abreast of the facts. (Proverbs 24:3-4 LB)

In summary, there is nothing incompatible between management and Christian principles or beliefs. Management is simply a means to an end and not an end in itself. In the church context, it is nothing more than a collection of tools and techniques devised by God-given human ingenuity to enhance human potential in the implementation of God's program and plan. And it is relevant for application to the ministries of the church, as well as to its administrative functions.

Chapter 5

Purposes

One of the interesting stories coming out of the Korean War is that of a mechanically minded man by the name of Wahlstrom. He enjoyed going to Army surplus sales and buying various intricate electrical and engineering instruments. He would carry them home, take them apart, and put them back together in unique and different combinations. After awhile he had filled an entire room in his home with various sized cogwheels, ringing bells, and lights. As one entered the room, one could push a button, and small, intricate wheels would start to turn. Gradually they would mesh with other wheels until all around the room wheels would be turning and whirring. As the last wheel moved into motion, a light would go on and gradually other lights would intermittently begin to flash on and off throughout the room until the room was lit up like a Christmas tree. As the final lights went on, a bell would begin to ring, and then other bells, until soon the entire room was filled with whirring wheels, flashing lights, and ringing bells. People were fascinated with the mechanical masterpiece and began to view Wahlstrom as a wonder. One of the townspeople nicknamed the machine Wahlstrom's Wonder. Its fame became widespread, and people began to come from miles around to view Wahlstrom's Wonder.

One day a visitor, impressed by the intricate mechanical responses to the push of a simple button, said to Mr. Wahlstrom, "This is really fascinating, but what does it do?" Mr. Wahlstrom explained, "Well, when you push the button the wheels turn, the lights flash, and the bells ring." The man replied, "Yes, I can see that, but what does it do?" And Mr. Wahlstrom replied again, "Well, you push a button, the wheels turn and . . ." In the face of the activity of this mechanical wonder, the question still remained: What function does it perform? What does it do?[1]

It is also possible for the church to become so engrossed in activities that sight of its real purposes becomes clouded or lost. This brings us to the subject of purposes, mission statements, objectives, goals, targets, visions! What do they all mean? Unfortunately, different things to different people, and, to add to the confusion, these terms are often used interchangeably. To keep it simple, we will be using just two of them—purposes and objectives—and defining our intended meaning for each.

Foundational to any ministries management system is a clear statement of what the ministries are intended to accomplish. More specifically, the basic purposes for which the church exists must be defined in specific terms. This sounds simple enough, yet clear statements of purpose are often the exception, and the implications to church ministries can be profound. Without clear direction, churches drift aimlessly, making it impossible to stir the congregation with a sense of expectation, excitement, and involvement. "Where there is no vision, the people perish" (Proverbs 29:18 KJV)—and we might add, churches stagnate and wither.

People want to belong to something that has a sense of purpose and direction. In pursuing a vision or purpose for the church, as well as for your personal life, seven "nevers" have been suggested by Rick Kingham, senior pastor of Overlake Christian Church, Redmond, Washington, a megachurch with attendance of over 5,000.

1. Never allow the world, the flesh, or Satan to shake your vision.
2. Never allow smallness of vision to rule your life.
3. Never allow those of no faith to influence you.
4. Never allow discouragement to dominate your faith.
5. Never allow circumstances to discourage your vision.
6. Never allow finances to dictate the vision.
7. Never allow failure to set your course in life.

With this visionary attitude, it is vital that the church leadership determine and communicate to the congregation what it believes to be God's direction in terms of basic purposes for the church, and to do so with a sense of boldness and expectation. In embarking upon such an effort, with the intent of ultimately launching a purpose-oriented ministries management system, it is important to prepare the congregation, as well as the church leadership, for what to many may be a new way of thinking. Such preparation might take several forms. Sending the church board or key leaders to a seminar that effectively communicates such an approach is a good way to get the church leadership on board. Rick Warren, author of *The Purpose-Driven Church* conducts seminars that may be helpful in this regard. For information, contact Saddleback Seminars, 1-800-633-8876. A series of messages to the congregation by the pastor on the purposes of the church and the need to emphasize ministries that fulfill these purposes in today's culture is a good way to prepare the congregation, including the church leadership.

In defining purposes, there is a tendency to intermingle purposes for the church with purposes from an individual perspective. There is an important distinction. Church purposes translate into specific ministries or programs. Individual purposes translate into a lifestyle that demonstrates the character of Christ, as well as actions that reflect this character. For example, if a church seeks to emphasize a greater evangelistic outreach through the lives of its members, the role or *direct* purpose of the church as an organization is a specific type of discipleship training, even though the ultimate outcome sought, or the indirect purpose, is more personal evangelism by its members. From the individual perspective, on the other hand, the purpose of such training and the role of the individual is evangelism by more effectively sharing one's faith. In defining purposes for the church in the context of ministries management concepts discussed later, it is important that church purposes be defined from this *direct* purpose and ministries-oriented perspective.

Once purposes are established, objectives are then defined in terms of specific programs or ministries to carry them out. This involves a process of reviewing current programs and ministries in the context of defined purposes; identifying voids, inadequacies, and/or imbalances; and then taking corrective steps. Program objectives is the subject of a later chapter, however, so further discussion will be deferred.

Definitions of purposes should be substantially more definitive than broad generalized statements such as: "Proclaiming the gospel of the Lord Jesus Christ to all nations." Such a general proclamation may represent good intent, but it is not theologically comprehensive (Scripture suggests much more in terms of purposes) and certainly does not lend itself to the formulation of a definitive ministries plan. Instead, specific statements of purpose should be established for each intended area of ministry.

Particularly important, purposes for the church ought to be based on Scripture that is perceived to reflect the heart of God. A good place to start might be the Great Commandment (Matthew 22:36-40) and the Great Commission (Matthew 28:19-20). These passages alone suggest what many churches might endorse as their purposes (really purpose categories), namely: Worship and celebration ("Love the Lord your God with all your heart, soul, and mind." Matthew 22:37 LB); mutual support and encouragement within the local body, and helping those in need—both church members and those in the community ("Love your neighbor as much as you love yourself . . . " Matthew 22:39 LB); evangelism ("Therefore go and make disciples in all the nations . . ." Matthew 28:19 LB); and discipleship (". . . and then teach these new disciples to obey all the commands I have given you . . ." Matthew 28:20 LB). Please note: this list of possible purposes is suggested only as an example to illustrate how purposes can and should be broken down sufficiently to accommodate responsive ministries. They may or may not be representative of the purposes that your church deems to be appropriate. Your church may have more or fewer purposes, including some of an entirely different nature. Purposes should be action-oriented. To illustrate, using the example purpose categories mentioned above, each might be described by a verb, as in the following: worship and celebration: *exalt;* mutual support and encouragement: *bond* people; evangelism: *bring* people; discipleship: *build* people.

Purposes can be influenced by how the church views itself in relation to American culture. Jimmy Long in *Generating Hope: A Strategy for Reaching the Postmodern Generation,*[2] defines five possible perspectives: the *assimilating church*, the *protecting church*, the *unchanging church*, the *battling church*, and the *influencing church*. The first three can be readily dismissed as being formulas for stagnation and decline. The *assimilating church* seeks to remain relevant to prevailing culture by adapting to some of its characteristics, but instead typically ends up being assimilated by the culture rather than influencing it. The *protecting church* seeks to withdraw from worldly influences, cocoon fashion, viewing the culture as beyond saving. But its isolationist bunker mentality and protection approach concerning cultural influences conflict with the outreach role of the church and make it destined to fail in today's information-oriented and interrelated society. The *unchanging church* is characterized by Long as one that just ignores culture and tries to hold on to its own traditions by rising above culture. His conclusion: "The unchanging church will be unable to draw in new members and will continue to lose its youth who feel the church has no answers for their struggles" (p. 1935). The remaining two perspectives, on the other hand, represent more valid considerations in terms of defining purposes. The *battling church* is committed to fighting a cultural war. Organizations such as Focus on the Family, the Christian Coalition, and the Family Research Council urge their constituents and supporting churches to resist the growing immorality and political influences that conflict with or erode traditional Judeo-Christian values by taking a more proactive posture. Long cites several areas of disagreement by many Christians with this perspective, including the appropriateness of a political role by the church, the erroneous presumption that all Bible-believing Christians are committed to the ideals of the Christian Right, and the apparent lack of success of the Christian Coalition and like-minded churches in attracting large numbers of younger people (Generation X). Those who dispute criticism of a *battling church* role compare such attitudes with that of the German church during the World War II Holocaust. The church's withdrawal from any role to resist political changes that undermine the basic Judeo-Christian values of society and which underscore the nation's greatness is "to fiddle while Rome burns" in the minds of *battling church* proponents. While most churches reject excessive emphasis on such a role, many endorse some type of ministry that informs and encourages a Christian citizenship response to political issues that undermine traditional moral values. Lastly, the *influencing church* is characterized as being in the world but not of the world. Instead of viewing the culture as a battlefield, it is seen as an outreach opportunity or mission field. The emphasis is to become intimately involved in the culture by befriending individuals with the gospel. Many view this perspective as being the most valid for today's environment.

Based on the preceding rationale and disregarding the first three from serious consideration (the *assimilating church,* the *protecting church,* and the *unchanging church*), the *battling church* and the *influencing church* concepts are relevant to the influence of purpose definition.

For example, churches that endorse the *battling church* concept might consider political activism within the bounds of tax-exempt status constraints to be a valid purpose. It might be termed something like "Sociopolitical Influence on Moral Issues" and imply a role for the church in such matters as: disseminating information to the congregation on national and local legislation, programs, and events that have moral or family values implications; or facilitating and encouraging active involvement of church members in civic, political, social, and other events or programs where moral or family values are relevant and where such involvement can exert a positive Christian influence. Advocates of such a purpose might cite Scripture that admonishes believers to be the salt of the earth and the light of the world (Matthew 5:13-16) and to overcome evil with good (Romans 12:21). Similarly, churches that embrace the *influencing church* perspective would likely include some variation of the previously referred to purpose categories, "Mutual Support and Encouragement" and "Community Outreach and Service."

So purposes will differ by church. Recognizing this, the purposes suggested earlier (worship, evangelism, discipleship, mutual support and encouragement, and community outreach and service) will be used throughout the book as representative examples in order to illustrate the concepts discussed. But this does not in any way imply that they are a preferred or appropriate list for most churches.

An important part of defining purposes is to go beyond general purpose categories, such as those mentioned above, and elaborate on them sufficiently to fully cover the intended meaning, intent, and scope. The scriptural basis for their selection should also be provided. No attempt is made to include such elaboration here, since we are describing a process or system. In addition to scriptural interpretation, purposes and the relative emphasis to be placed on each will differ for churches and be influenced by the communities they serve and the makeup of their congregations. Chapter 2 has provided some insight into social and cultural issues or trends that may prove helpful in this regard.

In group discussions on purposes, theological "donnybrooks" that serve no useful purpose should be avoided. To illustrate, using the example purpose categories mentioned earlier, Elder Petty might observe:

> Evangelism is the sole purpose of the church. That's the only reason God leaves us here after we're converted. And all other ministries or so-called purposes (i.e., worship, discipleship, mutual support and encouragement, and community service) are really means to an end, the end being evangelism. After all, discipleship and mutual encouragement serve the purpose of training and motivating Christians to more effectively communicate their faith, translating indirectly to the purpose of evangelism through personal witnessing. Similarly, community outreach and service has evangelism as its underlying purpose in that it seeks to attract the unchurched into the church and exposure to the gospel. And worship is key to an enhanced prayer life and a close walk with God, both essential for the Holy Spirit to use the individual as an effective witness—again, evangelism being the root purpose.

This rationale by Elder Petty illustrates the point made earlier in this chapter about confusing indirect purposes or outcomes with direct purposes of the church. Even though the purposes listed, other than "evangelism," may lead indirectly to some evangelism through lifestyle changes of the individuals impacted by their effective implementation, the direct purpose of each is not evangelism. Rather, evangelism is one of the fallout benefits, or byproducts. The purpose labeled "evangelism," on the other hand, refers to this purpose in the direct, rather than indirect, sense. Direct evangelism refers to church programs that are structured for evangelistic outreach through direct confrontation either on a group or individual basis. In an earlier era this might have been evangelistic or revival services. Today, it is more likely to include a special monthly all-day youth program that attracts unchurched young people for a time of fun and games, followed by a presentation of the Gospel and invitation to receive Christ. Or, it might be a men's breakfast with a special speaker (e.g., sports celebrity) to attract unchurched men and which would incorporate an evangelistic challenge. Some churches employ the Sunday school as the primary means of evangelistic outreach through programming designed to place evangelism on a par with Bible study and education in terms of purpose and emphasis. Direct evangelism might also include laywitness training coupled with visitation programs, or a child evangelism ministry aimed at reaching unchurched children, utilizing the Good News Club format of Child Evangelism Fellowship.

Purposes of the church are usually interdependent and mutually supportive. To illustrate, we will use the aforementioned example purpose categories as being representative for most churches. These five purpose categories, once again, are worship, evangelism, discipleship, mutual support and encouragement (within the local body of believers), and community outreach and service. Before illustrating the interdependence of such typical purpose categories, a brief explanation concerning the intended meaning of some of them may be helpful. Worship, discipleship, and evangelism need little explanation, although, as described in later chapters, programming that is responsive to each is changing along with the cultural shifts evolving in American society. "Mutual support and encouragement" acknowledges that people want to feel a sense of belonging and are looking for love and acceptance. We all need support and encouragement of one type or another and the local church body is called upon to meet this need more than ever before. Sometimes this is referred to as ministering to the needs of the local church body, and may take many forms: friendship (people are seeking friends, not just a "friendly church"); emotional support during times of personal crisis; financial help; counseling; the sense of belonging to a community or enlarged "family"; social gatherings for fun and fellowship; or other types of help or social relationships to meet a variety of circumstances. We live in a time of broken homes, single moms, divorced parents, blended families, dysfunctional families, and employment uncertainty as technology brings about sweeping changes to what were once stable careers. And all of this in an era of growing "independence," as opposed to "interdependence." We hardly know our neighbors these days; relatives are often geographically dispersed; and the unprecedented mobility of society often means that our few close friends and family members in the area may soon move away. Romans 12:10 (LB) helps to reinforce the scriptural basis for this purpose category: "Love each other with brotherly affection and take delight in honoring each other." These same needs also exist, of course, for those outside of the local church body. The purpose category labeled "community outreach and service" is intended to reflect the assumption that the church leadership in our example has decided to reach beyond the church boundaries and into the surrounding community to respond to these needs where they are often even greater. It envisions this as a unique new outreach ministry.

Refer now to Exhibit 5.1 to see how these five typical purpose categories interrelate. As shown, evangelism ministries produce new

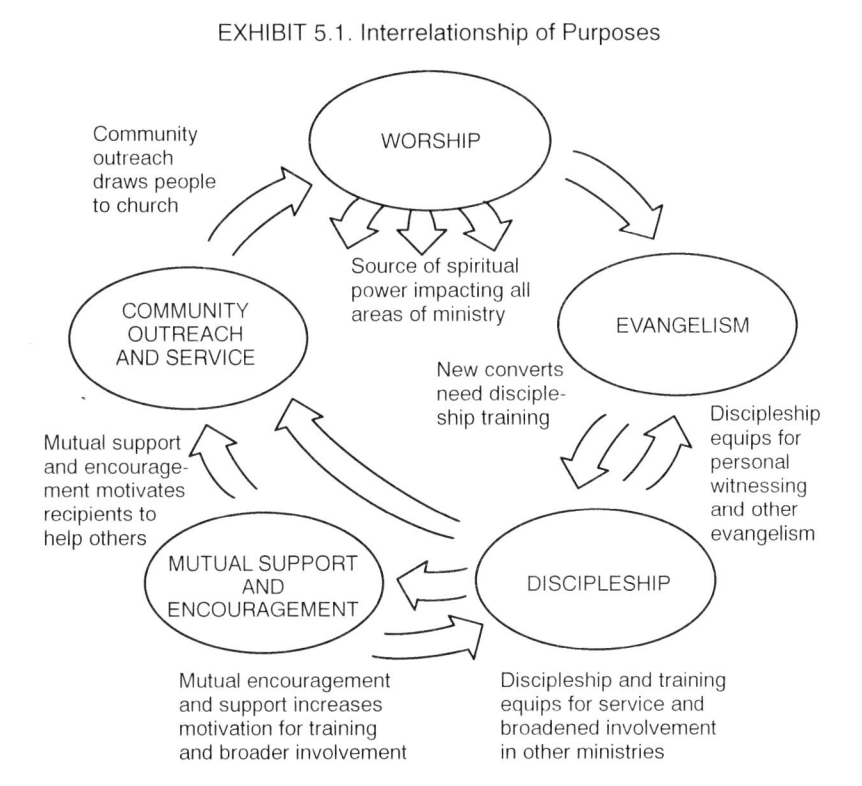

EXHIBIT 5.1. Interrelationship of Purposes

- Community outreach draws people to church
- Source of spiritual power impacting all areas of ministry
- New converts need discipleship training
- Discipleship equips for personal witnessing and other evangelism
- Mutual support and encouragement motivates recipients to help others
- Mutual encouragement and support increases motivation for training and broader involvement
- Discipleship and training equips for service and broadened involvement in other ministries

Nodes: WORSHIP, EVANGELISM, DISCIPLESHIP, MUTUAL SUPPORT AND ENCOURAGEMENT, COMMUNITY OUTREACH AND SERVICE converts, who then need to be discipled. As these new converts grow in spiritual maturity and are grounded in the faith through discipleship ministries, they become more effective personal witnesses, better equipped to win converts to Christ through a personal basis. Maturity in the faith through effective discipleship and training programs also leads those young in the faith to more involvement in other ministries of the church that fulfill other basic purposes. Mutual encouragement and support among members of the church body usually translates into greater personal commitment and involvement in church ministries. Similarly, as members are strengthened through interpersonal relationships or receive help to get back on their feet (emotionally, spiritually, or financially), they tend to have the compassion and desire to minister to others, including community outreach and service. Also, as their personal needs are fulfilled, they are likely to become more involved in other ministries of the church, which serve to fulfill various purposes. As the church reaches out to serve the community in various ways, such demonstrations of Christ's love will attract some into the church and to the Christian faith, and ultimately to their personal involvement in church affairs. And, finally, worship can be viewed as plugging into the power source that makes fulfillment of all of these purposes possible.

All this to say that basic purposes should not be viewed as independent stand-alones from one another, but rather as an interdependent and interrelated symphony of purposes that collectively provide the potential for synergistically extending the church ministry to new heights. By the same token, if one or more of the basic purposes is not fulfilled, it will probably have a detrimental impact on the fulfillment of others.

The preceding discussion has addressed purposes in terms of "what" they are. There is a second important dimension to purposes, namely "to whom" they are directed. Ministry purposes obviously focus on people, but to what type of people? People can be categorized in various ways, but the most useful way in terms of ministries is by age. Age gradation accommodates the differences in human interests, perspectives, mental abilities, and, often, values. The requirements for evangelism and discipleship, for example, are significantly different for children, teens, and adults. In defining and prioritizing church purposes, it is therefore important to specify not only the "what," but the "to whom."

THE MINISTRIES MATRIX

This brings us to the primary tool used in planning the ministries of the church in terms of fulfilling its basic purposes. It is called the Ministries Matrix, and is illustrated in Exhibit 5.2. Listed vertically on the left-hand side of the chart are the "what" in terms of basic purposes. This illustration uses the same hypothetical purpose categories discussed earlier. Remember, this is only an illustrative example. In real life, church leaders would determine the purposes that would be listed.

Horizontally across the top of Exhibit 5.2 is the other dimension important in defining purposes, the "to whom," or the age categories. As illustrated, the "to whom" in Exhibit 5.2 has been broken down into three basic age categories: children, youth, and adults. However, the adult category covers such a large age span, as well as age-based cultural diversity, that it needs to be subdivided into the different generational groups that largely comprise it: Generation X (also called the Baby Busters), the Baby Boomer generation, and those born prior to the Baby Boomers, sometimes called the Blazers and Builders. The Ministries Matrix in Exhibit 5.2 accommodates the possibility of twenty-five combinations of purposes and age categories. Hereafter, these are referred to as "mission categories."

A brief word is in order concerning foreign and domestic missions. The financial support of missionaries is certainly a valid purpose of the church. However, it would not be included as a purpose on the Ministries Matrix since management of the mission ministries falls under the jurisdiction of the missions board, not the local church. The local church role is largely one of screening candidates to be supported, fund-raising, budgeting, and dispensing support funds. A valid missions purpose in the ministries management context, however, could be to prepare and launch new missionaries. Such a purpose would typically translate into programs geared to providing increased missions awareness, challenging and motivating members concerning missions opportunities and needs, and providing training and information on various missions fields

EXHIBIT 5.2. Ministries Matrix

WHAT \ TO WHOM	CHILDREN (Under age 12)	YOUTH (Ages 13-18)	GENERATION X (Baby Busters)	BABY BOOMERS	PRE-BOOMERS
				ADULTS	
		PURPOSES OF THE LOCAL CHURCH			
WORSHIP	1	6	11	16	21
EVANGELISM	2	7	12	17	22
DISCIPLESHIP	3	8	13	18	23
MUTUAL SUPPORT & ENCOURAGEMENT	4	9	14	19	24
COMMUNITY OUTREACH & SERVICE	5	10	15	20	25

MISSION CATEGORIES

and missionary organizations. It also might involve short-term mission teams sent out and administered by the local church. Alternatively, such teams might be considered to be ministries under the purposes of evangelism or discipleship, depending upon the nature of their intended accomplishments.

Once the purposes of the church have been defined in the context of a Ministries Matrix in accordance with the preceding discussion, the next step, and the subject of the next chapter, is its use.

Chapter 6

Using the Ministries Matrix

The Ministries Matrix is a powerful management tool in ministries planning. It provides the mechanism for group dynamics in harnessing the collective wisdom of church leadership in formulating a ministries plan. It is a tool for bringing into focus the purposes and priorities of the church, evaluating current programming to determine whether it is in sync with these purposes and priorities, and providing a forum for the formulation of revised program plans. Using the Ministries Matrix involves a process that is quite simple, but effective. Its effectiveness stems from consensus agreement techniques and a systematic and disciplined approach to identifying and addressing important issues, rather than relying on intuitive judgment.

GETTING ORGANIZED

It is a good idea to begin by establishing a Ministries Matrix coordinator. The job of the coordinator is to facilitate the process of using the collective wisdom of the church board or designated leadership body—let's call it the leadership council—in accomplishing the intended planning and decision making. The coordinator should be someone who is also on the leadership council. Group dynamics stimulate creative thinking through the free exchange of ideas and opinions. Moreover, future plans must evolve through leadership consensus if they are to receive the broad acceptance and support necessary to succeed, particularly if substantial changes are involved. In this context, the role of the coordinator is to set the stage and facilitate such interchange. This involves introducing the concept, scheduling meetings, preparing agendas, leading discussions and keeping them on track, recording conclusions, and taking care of all the other support and administrative details involved.

The first job of the coordinator is to arrange for meetings in which the leadership council defines the basic purposes of the church, as discussed in Chapter 5. Once this has been accomplished, a Ministries Matrix similar to that of Exhibit 5.2 is prepared by or arranged for by the coordinator, incorporating the newly defined purposes of the church. However, in order to make the Ministries Matrix suitable as a visual display for group discussion forums, it needs to be enlarged sufficiently to provide good visibility and legibility for such use. The larger the group, the larger will be the size to satisfy this requirement. During the course of leadership council meetings in which the Ministries Matrix is used, information will be written on the mission category open squares of the matrix. Accordingly, it is a good idea to overlay the chart with transparent plastic sheeting so that such information can be readily erased and revised. Blank forms of the Ministries Matrix at the end of this book can be used to develop a blown-up version, provided there are companies in your area equipped to do this. Or you might find someone in your congregation with the artistic talent to draw a large version on chart-sized paper. Better yet, find a vacant wall in a meeting room, line a portion of the wall with blank paper using staples, tape, or other means of fastening, and create a large wall-size Ministries Matrix using artist's tape and flow pens. Three-foot wide rolls of grid paper are particularly useful because the faint blue grids facilitate taping or drawing horizontal and vertical lines, as well as providing guidelines for printing. Materials to do this are available at most art supply stores. The importance of a large wall chart version of the Ministries Matrix cannot be overstated. Everyone in the group needs to be focused on the same point during discussions and this cannot be done with everyone looking at individual 8½- by 11-inch copies. Nor is there sufficient room to record information in the mission category spaces. Moreover, the large wall-chart version provides the opportunity for leadership council members to individually stop by from time to time between meetings to review and mull over the information recorded, stimulating thought that will contribute to subsequent group meetings. This group-thinking concept using large wall-size displays, incidentally, is used extensively in the business world and is typically referred to as the "Depth Study" technique.

THE LEADERSHIP COUNCIL

As mentioned, the leadership council might be the church board or some other designated leadership body. Of paramount importance, however, is that it include an intergenerational balance. As discussed in Chapter 2, there are three generational groups in today's culture, in addition to Children and Youth. These are Generation X or the Baby Busters (born 1965-1984), the Baby Boomers (born 1946-1964), and the Pre-Boomers (born prior to 1946). If the church board is comprised entirely of Pre-Boomers, it will probably not have the necessary perspective concerning the younger generational groups. So, unless the church board has intergenerational representation, the leadership council should be enlarged to accommodate this need. It should also include representation that understands the needs of today's children and youth. The leadership council in this case is really a ministries committee that collectively has the balanced perspective of the entire age spectrum to which the church ministers or would like to minister.

In preparing the leadership council for the job they are to do, it is important to provide some type of preparatory instruction concerning the process they will be undertaking. The material in this book is intended for that purpose, and there are several excellent books listed at the end of this book that might be made available for reference, particularly those that deal with the different generational groups in greater depth. Each member of the leadership council needs to understand not only the process but also the information discussed in the earlier chapters concerning the different characteristics and ministry needs of Children, Youth, Generation Xers, Boomers, and Pre-Boomers. Information concerning establishing priorities and ministries that other churches have found to be successful should prove useful in preparing members of the leadership council for the job ahead.

SETTING PRIORITIES

Once the purposes have been defined and the preparations discussed previously are in place, a meeting of the leadership council should be convened to establish the relative priorities for each mission category. This is necessary because it is unlikely that all of the mission categories (the purposes by age categories) would be considered to be of equal importance. For example, suppose Elder Fossil suggests,

> Okay, now that we know our basic purposes and who we want to reach, let's agree on our priorities. I'm sure everyone recognizes that evangelism for adults represents our most critical mission categories right now. These are adults who are living Godless lives. Some are getting up in years and the time to reach them is slipping away. I propose we make this a top priority, appropriate most of our evangelism budget, and direct our primary evangelism programming emphasis toward reaching these men and women.

But suppose the youth sponsor disagrees.

> I'm not sure I agree with you, Bob. I think most of those adults, particularly the Boomers and Pre-Boomers, have had plenty of opportunities to respond to God's grace. I'm more concerned with reaching our youth. This is our last shot to influence them. Surveys show a high percentage leave the church in their later teen years. The kids today are really hurting and searching for meaning to life, and they have a whole lifetime ahead of them. I know I wish there had been a greater spiritual influence in my life when I was a teen. I think we need to spend our money on hiring a youth pastor who really understands this generation and who can relate to them and develop the kind of relationships and interchanges that will challenge them in their Christian faith.

Then the coordinator for the children's ministries interjects her views:

Now, wait a minute, gentlemen. I just read some statistics put out by Child Evangelism Fellowship and some other polls that show 85 percent of all people who become Christians make that commitment by the age of fourteen. Only 4 percent become Christians past the age of thirty. So, let's face it, the real opportunity for evangelism lies with children. I think that's where we need to put our top priority as far as evangelism is concerned. We need to get a Good News Club program going and we'll need all the new people we can get.

Similar responses of disagreement and options would be natural in any leadership council meeting or retreat. If a church had enough money, resources, people, and time, perhaps effective ministries in all of the mission categories could be managed. But churches do not have unlimited funds and volunteers. How does a church decide which mission categories in the Ministries Matrix to concentrate upon when considering the many opportunities they represent? Does the Bible say it is better to win children or youth to Christ over adults? Is it more effective to instill Christian values in a fourth-grader or a senior citizen? Often, the best balance of ministries is determined by the unique combination of circumstances and opportunities that confront each local church. The opportunities and needs related to a college community may not be the same as those related to either a residential or a retirement community. Similarly, the mission category priorities for a low-income, inner-city community might differ significantly from those of an affluent, middle-class area. The size of the church and the makeup of its congregation will also influence the priorities and type of ministries to be emphasized. For these reasons, churches do not have carbon copy ministries.

Serious thought is essential to making good decisions in this matter. In considering priorities, it is important to take into account the multigenerational and multicultural environment in which we live, as discussed in earlier chapters. The traditional two-parent family, stay-at-home moms, and a social environment that embraces traditional family values is no longer the norm. Much of the culture is now characterized by: broken homes; single moms and dads; divorced singles; latchkey kids; blended families; changed moral values; street kids; the decline or prohibition in teaching traditional values in public schools; the de facto endorsement of free sex among teens through safe sex curricula and condom distribution in public schools; the social acceptance of cohabitation; strong public and governmental pressure to accept politically correct social values; coed dorms in colleges and universities; the demonization of conservative Christians as extremists and homophobics; employment instability; social mobility; geographic dispersion of family members; the trend toward personal "independence" from the community as opposed to "interdependence"—and the list goes on and on. We have already addressed how much of this relates to changes ushered in by the Baby Boomer generation and the resulting impact of these changes upon Generation X and the Youth generations.

What are the implications of all this to the church and its ministries? The danger facing churches is the inertia that plagues all established social institutions in a rapidly changing socioeconomic environment. The tendency is to retain the traditional, resist the new, and lag in the adjustments necessary to remain relevant. The traditional programs of Sunday school, morning and evening worship, midweek Bible study and prayer, activity clubs, camp meetings, and the like, that some churches still see as filling basic ministry needs, are still wonderful programs. But they are also largely oriented toward stable, established Christians and their families, a society committed to traditional values, stable neighborhoods, and the economic environment of an era past. New programs to respond to the paradigm shifts of recent times are essential to supplement (not necessarily displace) such traditional ministries if the local church is to remain vibrant and alive. All this is mentioned to encourage those in leadership roles to move out from a prioritization mind-set that is unduly biased toward programs and ministries that were successful in an earlier era. Look seriously into "new horizon" purpose categories that imply the challenge of nontraditional programs that the church may never have tried before. But expect some objections if you do. I can hear Deacon Skeptic now:

> Just a minute now. Who's going to pay for all these new ministries you're trying to get us involved in—like this "Community Outreach and Service" stuff? Those people outside the church

don't make contributions, you know. It's fine for these guys that sit in ivory towers and write books, but down here where the rubber meets the road and where people like me administer the church budget, we need to know where the money is coming from.

Deacon Skeptic has a point. But it is a short-term perspective. If companies took this viewpoint, they would go out of business. It takes a company like Boeing four years or more to develop and launch a new commercial jet airplane. It takes about ten years to break even—or for the company to recover all of the money it has invested before it begins to realize a net gain. At the beginning of the jet age, Douglas, the leader in commercial aircraft at that time, decided to play it safe and stay with nonjet aircraft. Boeing took the plunge and entered the commercial aircraft market with the all-jet 707. The rest is history. Boeing is now the world's dominant commercial aircraft producer and Douglas is no longer on the scene (it was absorbed by Boeing in 1997 after it became McDonnell Douglas). Short-term versus long-term perspectives make a big difference. The same is true for the church. Deacon Skeptic just did not have the vision to see that reaching out through community service programs to the unchurched will, over time, produce spiritual dividends through the lives of individuals won to Christ through such outreach.

Hopefully, the material in Chapters 2 and 3 have helped to stimulate your thoughts in this regard. You may want to do some research on your own, as well, in determining priorities. This would be extremely desirable. In any case, take time to give the matter serious thought and prayer, and capitalize on the benefits of collective wisdom.

The end result of these "priority meetings" is to reach a consensus as to the relative priority of each mission category on the Ministries Matrix and to code each, using either color coding or symbols such as the following:

● High Priority
○ Medium Priority
Low Priority (no symbol)

If there is no interest at all in a given mission category, the words "no priority" would be written on the applicable mission category space. It may be that the leadership council will decide that there is no difference in priorities among the various mission categories. In that case, the coding for priority ratings can be dispensed with. Even this would represent a conscious decision that will influence how the ministries of the church are structured. Exhibit 6.1 illustrates how the Ministries Matrix would look with priority ratings coded in for each mission category for a hypothetical church. Let's call it Grace Church. Note that the leadership council for Grace Church has decided that quite a few of the mission categories merit a high priority rating—thirteen in all. Six were determined to be of medium priority, and six of low priority.

RECORDING CURRENT PROGRAMMING ON THE MINISTRIES MATRIX

With the Ministries Matrix now properly set up and mission categories prioritized, the next step is to simply write in each current program or ministry of the church on the Ministries Matrix in the mission category spaces to which each applies. In doing this, it would be helpful to first make a list of all present ministries or programs, identifying the basic purpose that each fulfills and for which age category—basically, the applicable mission category. This can best be done using a large chalkboard or chart to facilitate group discussion by the leadership council. As each program is identified and categorized as to applicable purpose and age group, it would also be an appropriate time to discuss the effectiveness of each program as it is listed. Exhibit 6.2 illustrates what all this might look like for Grace Church. Again, this interim step can be bypassed and the programs listed directly on the Ministries Matrix as shown later in this chapter. However, whether or not a chart like Exhibit 6.2 is used, it helps to illustrate the thought process that takes place before the programs or ministries are recorded on the Ministries Matrix. A blank copy of the Exhibit 6.2 form is included at the end of the book and can be enlarged or duplicated formatwise, if desired.

EXHIBIT 6.1. Ministries Matrix—Grace Church

PURPOSES OF THE LOCAL CHURCH

WHAT \ TO WHOM	CHILDREN (Under age 12)	YOUTH (Ages 13-18)	GENERATION X (Baby Busters)	BABY BOOMERS	PRE-BOOMERS
WORSHIP	● 1	● 6	● 11	● 16	● 21
EVANGELISM	● 2	● 7	● 12	○ 17	22
DISCIPLESHIP	3	● 8	○ 13	● 18	23
MUTUAL SUPPORT & ENCOURAGEMENT	4	○ 9	● 14	● 19	○ 24
COMMUNITY OUTREACH & SERVICE	5	○ 10	● 15	○ 20	25

CODE: ● High Priority ○ Medium Priority Low Priority (no symbol)

EXHIBIT 6.2. Listing of Current Ministries—Grace Church

AGE CATEGORY	CURRENT PROGRAM	PURPOSE CATEGORY		PROGRAM EFFECTIVENESS			
		PRIMARY	SECONDARY	CHILD-REN OR YOUTH	GEN. X	ADULTS BABY BOOMERS	PRE-BOOMERS
CHILDREN MINISTRIES	Sunday School	Evangelism	Discipleship	Good			
	Children's Church	Worship		Good			
	VBS	Evangelism		Good			
YOUTH MINISTRIES	Sunday School	Discipleship	Evangelism	Good			
	Youth Choir	Discipleship		Good			
	Activity Clubs	Discipleship	Evangelism	Good			
ADULT MINISTRIES	Adult/Youth Sunday Worship	Worship		Poor	Poor	Fair	Good
	Sunday School	Discipleship			Fair	Fair	Fair
	Midweek Program	Worship Discipleship			Poor	Good	Fair
	Choir	Worship	Mutual Support		Good	Good	Good
	Counseling	Mutual Support	Community Outreach		Good	Good	Fair
	Teacher Training	Discipleship			Good	Good	Fair
	Home Fellowships	Mutual Support	Discipleship		Good	Good	Good
	Food Bank	Community Outreach			Good	Good	Good

Referring to the list compiled by Grace Church (Exhibit 6.2), note that some of the ministries on this list have been judged to be oriented about equally toward two purpose categories ("Youth Activity Clubs" and the "Adult Midweek Program"). Some are oriented primarily toward one, but also contribute significantly to a lesser or secondary degree to another. In compiling such a list it is important to use good discretion when indicating a secondary focus for ministries beyond the purpose for which they are primarily intended. A loose interpretation could have every ministry contributing in some sense to almost every purpose category. For example, the Sunday worship service obviously is oriented toward the "Worship" purpose category. But the position might be taken that it also contributes to the purpose categories "Discipleship" and "Evangelism" since the sermon content includes appeals to accept the Christian faith (Evangelism), as well as instruction concerning the Christian life and service (Discipleship). This type of "stretch" is not the intent. For a ministry to qualify as serving a secondary purpose in addition to its primary focus, the secondary application must be significant. Such instances should be the exception and usually not more than one secondary purpose application for a ministry.

As mentioned, in addition to a listing of current programs and the mission categories they are intended to fulfill, it would also be an appropriate time to evaluate and make a qualitative judgment as to the effectiveness of these current ministries. As noted on Exhibit 6.2, qualitative ratings of "good," "fair," or "poor" have been indicated for each. The rationale for the given ratings would be recorded in notes for use as described later. Note also that for the adult age group, a given ministry might be rated as "good" for one of the three adult age categories but "poor" or "fair" for another. For example, the "Midweek Program" for adults was rated "poor" for the Generation X category but "good" and "fair," respectively, for the Boomers and Pre-Boomers. The leadership council apparently concluded that a single program for these three adult age categories is not effective. They represent three different cultural paradigms and the needs for each differ. In this case, the program apparently is geared primarily to the older adult generations and is not fulfilling the requirements for an effective Generation X ministry.

This evaluation process should seek factual data to the extent possible. It should view programs in terms of the specifics that define the purpose they are intended to fulfill, not broad generalities. To illustrate, using "Discipleship" as an example, if part of the Discipleship purpose is defined as development that leads to personal evangelism, then statistics concerning how many new converts have joined the church during the past year ought to be a serious consideration. If little or no evangelism is taking place, then the overall rating of programs intended to fulfill this aspect of the Discipleship purpose ought to be graded accordingly. The grading should also take into account the extent to which other aspects of the Discipleship purpose are adequately or inadequately fulfilled. For example, the evangelism development aspect of the Discipleship purpose might be poor for a given program, but leadership training and Bible study might be judged to be very effective (assuming they are also defined as part of the Discipleship purpose). In other words, the program evaluation process should encompass performance considerations covering each element of the defined purpose. This process might include interviewing program leaders or those attending the programs to determine program effectiveness.

Note in Exhibit 6.2 that the leadership council of Grace Church has indicated that the "Youth Activity Clubs" ministry responds to two purpose categories on a primary basis and one on a secondary basis. The leadership council's judgment in this case reflects the fact that most of the young people who attend these clubs at Grace Church are members of the church family. They have been thoroughly exposed to Christian teaching and influence, and the primary emphasis maintained by the leaders in charge of this youth ministry has therefore been discipleship, Christian growth, and the mutual support, encouragement, and the sense of belonging that occurs through the various club activities and outings. However, the clubs also attract a smaller percentage of young people who are not affiliated with the church, and who do not have a Christian background. The program leaders make special effort to seek opportunities to introduce these young people to a personal faith in Christ, thereby providing a significant, although secondary, evangelistic component to the ministry as well.

Once the list of current ministries has been compiled, along with an indication of purpose orientation and an evaluation of effectiveness, each is recorded on the Ministries Matrix in the mission category to which it applies. Exhibit 6.3 shows how the ministries listed on Exhibit 6.2 for Grace Church would appear on their Ministries Matrix. The ministry, "Sunday Worship" would be entered in mission categories 6, 11, 16, and 21 on the Ministries Matrix since it responds to the purpose of "Worship" for both the youth and adult categories. A checkmark (✓) appearing after a ministry indicates that it contributes on a primary basis to the mission categories in which it appears. If no checkmark appears it indicates that it contributes on a secondary basis.

EVALUATING THE CURRENT MINISTRIES PLAN

The completed Ministries Matrix (Exhibit 6.3) is, in effect, the current ministries plan of Grace Church. The next step in the ministries planning process is for the leadership council to either endorse this current plan or decide that it needs to formulate a new plan to bring ministries more in sync with defined purposes and priorities. The leadership council would endorse the plan if it believes that current programming responds adequately to the purposes and priorities defined for the church. Otherwise, it needs to evaluate where the current plan is deficient and formulate a new ministries plan. Consider the typical thought process and conclusions that might be expected as the leadership council of Grace Church meets to consider its newly completed Ministries Matrix in the context of the effectiveness ratings indicated on Exhibit 6.2. These two charts used together provide the basis for them to do this. The Ministries Matrix highlights the extent to which current ministries exist or are absent in prioritized mission categories, while the Exhibit 6.2 chart summarizes the adequacy and effectiveness of existing ministries. Together they provide the visibility and basis for determining future ministry changes and strategies.

At first glance, the council is encouraged that most of the high and medium priority mission categories shown on the Ministries Matrix appear to have responsive programming. But there are also some glaring voids. Six of the mission categories have no programming at all (numbers 4, 5, 10, 12, 17, and 22). One of these is rated a high priority (number 12), two a medium priority (numbers 10 and 17), and three a low priority (numbers 4, 5, and 22). In addition, there

EXHIBIT 6.3. Ministries Matrix—Grace Church

WHAT \ TO WHOM	CHILDREN (Under age 12)	YOUTH (Ages 13-18)	GENERATION X (Baby Busters)	BABY BOOMERS	PRE-BOOMERS
WORSHIP	1 ● Children's Church/	6 ●	11 ● Sunday Worship Service/ Midweek Prayer/Bible Study/ Adult Choir/	16 ●	21
EVANGELISM	2 ● Sunday School/ VBS/	7 ● Sunday School Activity Clubs	12 ●	17 ○	22
DISCIPLESHIP	3 ● Sunday School	8 ● Sunday School/ Youth Choir Activity Clubs	13 ○ Sunday School Classes/ Midweek Prayer/Bible Study/ Teacher Training/ Home Fellowships	18 ●	23
MUTUAL SUPPORT & ENCOURAGEMENT	4	9 ○ Activity Clubs/	14 ● Adult Choir/ Counseling/ Home Fellowships/	19 ●	24 ○
COMMUNITY OUTREACH & SERVICE	5	10 ○	15 ● Counseling/ Food Bank/	20 ○	25

CODE: ● High Priority ○ Medium Priority Low Priority (no symbol) are indications from Exhibit 6.2 ratings of current ministries that several may need some level of reorientation to improve their effectiveness.

What must happen next is a discussion by the leadership council concerning each mission category to determine the adequacy of current programming for each. The resulting output will be a consensus decision concerning which categories require new programs and whether some of the existing programs need to be reoriented. These decisions will not include the specifics of such new programming at this point, but simply the need. Follow-up studies will be required to consider program options and ultimate selection.

This discussion by the leadership council is extremely important. What has been accomplished thus far is problem identification. The Ministries Matrix has been used to precipitate a systematic evaluation to provide visibility as to where discrepancies exist between the purposes the leadership has defined for the church and the reality of current programming. The Ministries Matrix, together with the Exhibit 6.2 chart, does not provide the answers but does set the stage for that to happen. Problem definition is the first step to problem solution.

After going over the Ministries Matrix and discussing each mission category, the leadership of Grace Church would summarize its findings. Exhibit 6.4 illustrates what their typical thought process and conclusions might look like.

Exhibit 6.5 shows the completed Ministries Matrix with the mission categories labeled "problem" that either need new programs or some type of reorientation of existing ministries. The bottom line for Grace Church is that to adequately fulfill all of the mission categories that it has defined for itself using the Ministries Matrix, it would need to launch about eight new programs and reorient several others.

This all boils down to the realization for Grace Church that it is currently a long way from where it wants to be in terms of ministries outreach. The church currently has a total of fourteen ministries or programs. Adding eight new ones along with some reorientation of others equates to a 50 to 60 percent ministries increase. At this point, Grace Church needs to make some important decisions concerning future ministries strategy and to develop a ministries plan. Strategy possibilities in this regard are outlined in the next chapter, along with a typical strategy plan that might evolve for Grace Church in view of the conclusions reached.

EXHIBIT 6.4. Typical Thought Process by Grace Church Leadership Council

Mission
Category **Children Ministries**

1. *Worship:* High priority category. Has well-run children's church. No changes necessary.
2. *Evangelism:* High priority. Sunday school is a good program with an evangelism emphasis but reaches only churched children. Vacation Bible School is also a good program and reaches unchurched children, but is only two weeks out of the year. Strategic significance requires added programming to reach more unchurched children.
3. *Discipleship:* Sunday school is the only responsive program and discipleship is a secondary emphasis. Relatively weak programming for this category, but since it is a low priority no changes planned for now.
4. *Mutual Support & Encouragement:* No current programs for this low priority category. With the high divorce rate and large number of single parent families, many children are hurting. It was downgraded in priority only because of more urgent ministry needs. Same situation exists for mission category 5 (Community Outreach and Service). Nevertheless, we should consider at least one new program that would be responsive to both mission categories 4 and 5.
5. *Community Outreach & Service:* See category 4 comments above for program to jointly serve both categories 4 and 5.

Youth Ministries

6. *Worship:* High priority category. One-size-fits-all worship service for youth and adults is not satisfactory. Consider adding a contemporary worship service for youth and young adults.
7. *Evangelism:* High priority. Two good programs currently serve this category but evangelism is a secondary emphasis. Sunday school is geared to churched youth. The activity clubs include about 20 percent of unchurched youth. Strategic significance suggests need for added programming aimed toward unchurched youth.
8. *Discipleship:* High priority. Three strong programs currently in operation emphasizing discipleship. No changes needed.
9. *Mutual Support & Encouragement:* Medium priority. The youth activity clubs are currently doing a good job. No new programming appears necessary but reinforce existing programming if needed with funding and/or personnel to assure continued adequacy. Consider sending Youth Pastor to seminar or workshop to upgrade awareness on what other churches are doing.
10. *Community Outreach & Service:* Medium priority. Currently no programming to serve this category. Need new outreach program to minister to unchurched youth.

Generation X Ministries

11. *Worship:* High priority. Three programs currently serve this category but two of these are rated poor for this age group (worship service and midweek prayer and Bible study), which are geared formatwise to Boomers and Pre-Boomers. Consider adding contemporary worship service per category 6 discussion.

12. *Evangelism:* High priority. No current ministries. New programming needed. May be accommodated best through small group relational-oriented or seeker ministry.
13. *Discipleship:* Medium priority. Currently several strong programs in certain areas. However, little or no evangelism is taking place in the church or through the members. Since part of the defined purpose for discipleship is development of how to share faith and win others to Christ, this aspect is lacking. Need to reorient some of the programs to more emphasis and training in personal evangelism. Other aspects of discipleship (i.e., doctrinal teaching, Bible study, teacher training, etc.) appear to be well covered. One other problem is that the midweek program is geared to older generations. Need exists for a separate and different approach for Generation X.
14. *Mutual Support & Encouragement:* High priority. Currently several strong programs. No changes necessary.
15. *Community Outreach & Service:* High priority. Currently two strong programs, one with a secondary emphasis. Could use reinforcement with additional programming. Needs research as to how best to minister to the community and this age category.

Boomer Ministries

16. *Worship:* High priority. Adequately served through current programming.
17. *Evangelism:* Medium priority. No current programming. Need small group support type workshops to attract and minister to unchurched Boomers in need of help with personal problems (i.e., divorce, single parents, addictions).
18. *Discipleship:* High priority. Several strong programs currently serve this mission category but need evangelism component strengthened per item 13 comment, above.
19. *Mutual Support & Encouragement:* High priority. Three strong programs adequately accommodate this mission category. No new programming needed.
20. *Community Outreach & Service:* Medium priority. Two strong programs serve this category. Changes proposed for category 17, above, would provide additional reinforcement.

Pre-Boomer Ministries

21. *Worship:* High priority. Adequately served through current programming.
22. *Evangelism:* Low priority. No current programming. No new programming recommended at this point, but opening up home fellowships to include unchurched neighbors might be a possibility. Existing fellowship groups need to be challenged in this regard.
23. *Discipleship:* Low priority. Current programming is adequate except for strengthening evangelism component per item 14, above.
24. *Mutual Support & Encouragement:* Medium priority. Current programming is adequate. No new programming required.
25. *Community Outreach & Service:* Low priority. Current programming adequate at this time.

EXHIBIT 6.5. Ministries Matrix—Grace Church

WHAT \ TO WHOM	CHILDREN (Under age 12)	YOUTH (Ages 13-18)	GENERATION X (Baby Busters)	ADULTS — BABY BOOMERS	ADULTS — PRE-BOOMERS
WORSHIP	1 ● Children's Church / PROBLEM	6 ● PROBLEM	11 ● PROBLEM	16 ● Sunday Worship Service / Midweek Prayer/Bible Study / Adult Choir	21 ●
EVANGELISM	2 ● PROBLEM	7 ● PROBLEM	12 ● PROBLEM	17 ○ PROBLEM	22
DISCIPLESHIP	3 Sunday School	8 ● Sunday School / Youth Choir / Activity Clubs	13 ● PROBLEM	18 ● Sunday School / Midweek Classes / Bible Study / Training / Home Fellowships PROBLEM	23
MUTUAL SUPPORT & ENCOURAGEMENT	4 PROBLEM	9 ○ Activity Clubs	14 ●	19 ● Adult Choir / Counseling / Home Fellowships	24 ○
COMMUNITY OUTREACH & SERVICE	5 PROBLEM	10 ○ PROBLEM	15 ○	20 ● Counseling / Food Bank	25

CODE: ● High Priority   ○ Medium Priority   Low Priority (no symbol)

96

Chapter 7

Developing a Ministries Strategy

Effective change requires a strategy and a detailed plan to implement the strategy. Several types of possible strategies are discussed in the following sections. They are intended to be thought provoking but are by no means all inclusive. Many other possibilities and variations exist; excellent books are available on the subject, some of which are referenced at the end of this book. The best strategy will be influenced by church size, current congregational makeup in terms of generational categories (Pre-Boomers, Boomers, Generation Xers, and Youth), defined purposes of the church, the population characteristics of the community in which the church is located, and other circumstances unique to each church.

MULTIGENERATIONAL CENTRALIZED STRATEGY

This strategy consists of expanding the home base ministries to achieve a balanced outreach to all generational categories. This typically means adding new ministries to fill ministry voids and reorienting others as determined by the Ministries Matrix evaluation process. This is a centralized approach in that any expansion of or changes to ministries is accomplished at the home church, rather than through a decentralized approach, such as church planting, house churches, or alignments and cooperation with parachurch organizations.

This strategy is geared primarily to large and midsized churches for several reasons. The primary reason is that it takes a large church with the necessary resources to implement the strategy within a reasonable time frame. As previously mentioned, about half of all churches in the United States have congregations of 75 to 100 or less. These are classified as small churches for purposes of our discussion. About one out of four Protestant churches have congregations of 200 to 400. These can be considered to be midsize. Those with one thousand or more in attendance at weekend services constitute less than 3 percent of the total. Therefore, if size is a primary criterion, the strategy is probably oriented toward less than 25 percent of all churches, at most.

It might be presumed that most large or megasize churches are full-service oriented with a variety of ministries to reach all generational categories. This is true for some; but based on personal observation, others are oriented largely toward the Boomer and Pre-Boomer generations. The relative affluency of these generational categories that makes possible the financial resources to achieve and sustain large church status, can also influence a ministry agenda geared largely toward their interests and needs. This may not be by design and not even recognized until the Ministries Matrix exercise reveals a disconnect between the church's vision and its current programming. That is another reason why the Ministries Matrix evaluation process is important. Once a formal review is undertaken, it helps to reveal to churches that may feel quite comfortable and self-satisfied that they are actually falling short of the purposes to which they subscribe.

Referring back to our hypothetical Grace Church example, the Ministries Matrix analysis revealed the need for a 50 to 60 percent expansion in the number of ministries plus the reorientation of several others. That was the requirement to accommodate all of the mission categories that Grace Church defined as important in its vision to achieve a relatively broad multicultural ministries agenda. Most small churches would run into a similar problem if they sought to implement this type of broad-based centralized strategy. The broad multicultural ministries agenda, therefore, might be a good long-term vision for smaller churches, like Grace Church, but it is unrealistic for a near- to intermediate-term strategy.

TARGETED CENTRALIZED STRATEGY

A second option, and one that would probably be more appropriate for Grace Church, is to narrow the focus in terms of purposes, priorities, and generational outreach. In short, adopt a targeted approach. This accommodates the reality that all churches cannot be all things to all people, as discussed in Chapter 3, on the subject of church size as it relates to priorities. Since Boomers are drawn to large churches that provide the variety and benefits of a full-service agenda, which small churches cannot provide, it may be logical for some churches to turn their focus on the Youth and Generation X categories. This strategy allows the small church to more adequately minister to fewer generational categories by concentrating its limited resources on such targeted groups. Established churches would, of course, continue to accommodate the Pre-Boomers, who probably constitute its primary base of support, as well as others who desire to attend, but its priorities would be focused and more responsive to some generational categories than to others. The difficulties and challenges faced by established smaller churches under this strategy have already been discussed in Chapter 3. However, it remains a viable strategy for those that have a pastor and leadership with a vision toward the future and the courage to launch out in new directions. It also requires a congregation that shares in this vision. Start-up churches do not have the same problem as established churches. They can be launched with an agenda that is totally oriented toward a specific generational category. As the church grows, it can expand its outreach and target other generational categories, as well.

SMALL GROUPS STRATEGY

This is also a targeted strategy that can work well with churches of small to large size. Rick Warren in *The Purpose-Driven Church*[1] advocates small groups that have a specialized purpose. Such purpose-oriented small groups include:

1. *Seeker groups:* formed for evangelism by providing a non-threatening environment for nonbelievers to ask questions and explore the Christian faith
2. *Service groups:* formed to perform a special ministry
3. *Growth groups:* geared to Bible study and discipleship training
4. *Support groups:* formed for the purpose of fellowship and mutual support for specific needs.

Warren identifies new parents, college students, empty nesters, recovery groups, and those with specific hurts as typical types of special-need support groups. As discussed in Chapter 2, different types of small groups are appropriate for different generational categories. Generation Xers crave the intimate community of a small group that provides the sharing over time through activities that extend beyond meetings and which build close relationships. Baby Boomers are drawn to support groups that minister during the transition times of their lives, such as divorce, remarriage, unemployment, death of a parent, etc. Pre-Boomers often seek fellowship and Bible study. Various generational categories respond to service and growth-oriented support group ministries.

Large churches have the resources to implement a broad array of support groups as a strategy to respond to a number of mission categories. Smaller churches must employ a more selective approach, targeting specific generational groups. Grace Church, for example, might seek to expand its outreach to Generation Xers through seeker and small support groups. These small group ministries could be implemented without revamping the more traditional ministry agenda of the church, except that it would likely involve adding a second worship service that is contemporary in format. Accordingly, it is a valid strategy, even for small established churches, where reorientation of the traditional core ministries would be a hard sell to a tradition-oriented congregation.

SATELLITE CHURCHES

An effective strategy for mid- to large-size churches is to launch satellite churches. This decentralized strategy may be a better choice than seeking to achieve a multigenerational outreach internally, taking into account pastoral strengths, congregation makeup, resources constraints, leadership orientation, and similar factors. It is an alternative approach to reaching markets that the church might otherwise find difficult to accommodate in context with internal versus external demands. Ministry requirements for internal (congregation) and external (unchurched) markets are often very different. We tend to feel that churches should cover the market spectrum through home-base ministries. But some churches may find it more practical to launch satellite ministries that target certain generational groups. Moreover, it might actually be a better strategy for fulfilling some of the defined purposes by reaching unchurched individuals who would otherwise be difficult to attract in a more traditional large church setting.

One example of this is a new independent church in our area that was launched just one year before the date of this writing. Real Life Church of Maple Valley, Washington, was started under the leadership of the youth pastor of a large evangelical church. The young pastor, who had led the youth ministry for about fourteen years, had a burden to reach the younger unchurched segment of his own generation and others who either had no Christian experience in their background or who were, for one reason or another, disenchanted with "conventional Christianity." Coming from a dysfunctional family background himself and having experienced many of the frustrations and unfortunate life experiences of his generation, the pastor was able to empathize with the younger generation's cultural orientation, needs, and perspective. To make a long story short, he left the home church with the blessings and encouragement of the senior pastor and the congregation, as well as with a small cadre of about twenty-five supporters who wanted to assist in the new church start-up effort. They received modest home church financial sponsorship for about a year and, through an aggressive door-to-door visitation outreach with "door hanger" literature about the church, it took off quite rapidly. Attendance also has been helped by local newspaper articles reporting on some of the volunteer community projects that the church undertakes from time to time. It currently meets in rented public school facilities, grew to a congregation of about 275 in its first year, continues to grow rapidly, and has a broad base of ministries. These include a variety of community outreach and assistance programs, a new youth center with some nonconventional youth programs, and a missionary outreach to Guatemala. In addition to financial support, a team of members goes to a Guatemalan orphanage periodically to assist in construction activities and needed repair work. The church is attended largely by Generation Xers. The appeal is not eloquent preaching, but a caring church that is ministering to mostly younger adults and youth who have failed to find spiritual fulfillment or acceptance in more traditional ministry settings. One of their announced goals as they entered their second year was to focus increasingly on children and youth, with the emphasis not on numbers but on ministering to needs on an individual basis. In so doing, the growth in numbers seems to occur automatically.

As suggested from the preceding case study, the role of the sponsoring church under this strategy is to provide the initial staff, a nucleus of start-up members, and financial support for a limited period of time. As mentioned, this is a suitable strategy for mid- to large-sized churches. A variation for very large churches is to launch satellite churches oriented toward a broad generational spectrum, rather than the more generationally targeted approach described here. A good example of this variation is Overlake Christian Church of Redmond, Washington. This church of about 5,000 attendees has launched eight new satellite churches in the greater Seattle area over the past decade, each of which typically starts up with several hundred members from the parent congregation. Each has flourished from the outset.

HOUSE CHURCH STRATEGY

A modified decentralized approach is planting house churches, which maintain a close connection with the mother church. Under this concept small groups of people with common interests and generation-based cultural orientation are formed and meet during the week in homes for Bible study, prayer, and sharing. Trained leaders are provided by the mother church to ensure doctrinal integrity, direction, and general oversight. The house churches might gather together Sunday evenings at the mother church for a joint contemporary service of music, testimonies, and teaching or preaching. Functions carried on by each house church would typically include the recruitment and assimilation of unchurched newcomers, evangelism, Bible study, disciple making, pastoral care, mutual support and encouragement, and special community service projects. The mother church would still maintain its traditional ministries, including morning worship services, Sunday school, midweek programs, etc., primarily for those not enrolled in one of the house churches but also open to house church members. This concept is a hybrid strategy with both centralized and decentralized aspects. It embodies the more intimate and informal "extended family" setting that appeals to much of the younger generational categories, as discussed in Chapter 2. At the same time it provides for stability, doctrinal integrity, and the option of opportunities for special ministries involvement and youth activities offered by the mother church that would not be feasible by the house churches on their own. Further, it continues to accommodate those who find the more traditional church format desirable. House churches can provide a means of transition to traditional church involvement for those who are unchurched and who might find assimilation directly into a traditional church difficult.

TRADITIONAL AND CONTEMPORARY SERVICES STRATEGY

The University Presbyterian Church of Seattle, Washington, has found an effective ministries formula for the multigenerational makeup of its congregation. This large church has about 4,000 members. The church conducts three identical Sunday morning services. These are traditional in nature and are geared largely to Boomers and Pre-Boomers. The church also holds two identical Sunday evening services, both of which are geared to the Youth and Generation X categories, which include the college-age crowd. The church is near the University of Washington and the two Sunday evening services are packed with college students and young people. The evening services feature contemporary music, audience participation, and interchange in various ways, including prayer requests made through a roving microphone, and the same message from the senior pastor that is given at the morning services. The evening message might be varied slightly in presentation to accommodate the younger age level, but the basic message is essentially the same. A time of fellowship and snacks takes place between the two evening services. This makes it clear that there is no need to compromise the message in ministering to younger generations. However, the worship service format is an extremely important factor in such outreach. Church size is not necessarily a constraint to this strategy.

GRACE CHURCH STRATEGY

Now let us turn our attention back to Grace Church. You recall that in the preceding chapter it was determined from the Ministries Matrix evaluation that ten mission categories represented "problem" areas. That is, based on the priorities by mission category originally established by the leadership council, ten of the mission categories were deficient in terms of responsive programming. To correct this, eight new programs would be needed along with some reorientation of several others. Based on these findings, a typical rationale and resulting strategy might be expected to evolve along the following lines.

1. The ministries expansion, called for by the Ministries Matrix evaluation and based upon the priorities established for each mission category, was concluded to be more than the church could handle, at least for the near to intermediate term.
2. Accordingly, a decision was made to redefine priorities using a more targeted approach. More specifically, it was agreed to retain the priorities originally established for the Youth, Generation X, and Pre-Boomer categories, but to de-emphasize the Baby Boomer category. The priorities for all Baby Boomer mission categories were therefore dropped to low and no new programs would be launched for low priority mission categories. This rationale was based on the conclusion that Grace Church was not currently large enough to provide an effective outreach to the Boomer generation, and that by narrowing its focus somewhat, it could substantially upgrade its outreach to the Youth and Generation X categories.
3. Based on this rationale and previously determined ministry voids, it was decided to launch the following new programs:
    a. A *contemporary evening worship service*, geared to Youth and Generation Xers, much along the lines described earlier in this chapter under "Traditional and Contemporary Services Strategy."
    b. A *Good News Club program* designed to evangelize unchurched children through home-based weekly Bible clubs, similar to the program described in Chapter 3 under "Children."

c. The establishment of a *Youth Center*. This would be a recreational program open to neighborhood youth. It would include use of the church's multipurpose facility for scheduled sporting events and clinics, pool tournaments, and other activities attractive to young people. It would seek to respond to the mission categories of *evangelism* as well as *community outreach and service* to youth. The emphasis would be to provide wholesome recreational opportunities to unchurched and churched neighborhood youth with the objective of using such opportunities to introduce them to the Christian faith, provide assistance with personal problems, and gradually encourage their involvement in other church activities and attendance.

d. Establish a *small group seeker* program. The objective is evangelism directed toward Generation Xers. The format would be small group meetings that provide a nonthreatening environment for unchurched young men and women to explore the Christian faith through questions where they could seek answers to their doubts. The follow-up would include inviting their attendance at the small group home fellowships currently oriented toward this generation category.

4. Beyond these new programs, the Sunday school program for Generation X attendees would be reoriented to emphasize personal witnessing in terms of biblical foundation, methods, and personal obligation. The objective is more effective disciple building that leads to greater personal involvement in Christian outreach.

Collectively, these changes would result in the revised Ministries Matrix for Grace Church illustrated by Exhibit 7.1. The added programs are in italics. This revised matrix, in effect, represents the new ministries plan for Grace Church—one that is challenging but that the leadership council views to be achievable within a near- to intermediate-term time period. The revised Ministries Matrix and plan it represents no longer includes mission categories labeled "problem" since it is now responsive to the redefined purposes and priorities.

EXHIBIT 7.1. Ministries Matrix—Grace Church (Revised Plan)

PURPOSES OF THE LOCAL CHURCH

WHAT \ TO WHOM	CHILDREN (Under age 12)	YOUTH (Ages 13-18)	ADULTS — GENERATION X (Baby Busters)	ADULTS — BABY BOOMERS	ADULTS — PRE-BOOMERS
WORSHIP	1 ● Children's Church✓	6 ● ←—— Contemporary Worship✓ ——→	11 ●	16 ● Sunday School Classes✓ Midweek Prayer/Bible Study✓ Adult Choir✓	21 ●
EVANGELISM	2 ● Sunday School✓ VBS✓ Good News Club Program✓	7 ● Sunday School Activity Clubs Youth Center✓	12 ○ Small Group Seeker Ministry✓	17 ○	22
DISCIPLESHIP	3 Sunday School	8 ● Sunday School✓ Youth Choir Activity Clubs	13 ○	18 ● Sunday School Classes✓ Midweek Prayer/Bible Study✓ Teacher Training✓ Home Fellowships	23
MUTUAL SUPPORT & ENCOURAGEMENT	4	9 ○ Activity Clubs✓	14 ●	19 ● Adult Choir✓ Counseling✓ Home Fellowships✓	24 ○
COMMUNITY OUTREACH & SERVICE	5	10 ○ Youth Center✓	15 ●	20 ○ Counseling✓ Food Bank✓	25

CODE: ● High Priority   ○ Medium Priority   Low Priority (no symbol)

106

OTHER FOLLOW-UP ACTIVITIES

For any of the preceding strategies that call for the development of new programs or the reorientation of others, follow-up study and planning will be required concerning each of the mission categories involved. Preferably, present leaders of affected mission categories should be tapped to carry out this effort. For example, if it is determined that new programs or changes to current programs in the children ministry are called for, the present leaders of children ministries should be asked to do such follow-up planning, including determining required personnel, space, and cost. Their findings and recommendations would then be presented to the leadership council or the authority that replaces it.

After this has been done and specific new plans and/or programming objectives have been established, it is important to share the results and the vision of the leadership council with the congregation. This might be done at a special congregational meeting or church dinner. The work of the leadership council and its findings would be presented, using professional quality graphics and visual techniques. The purpose is to get everyone on board by enthusiastically presenting the church's new vision for future growth and outreach, and to elicit broad congregational support and involvement.

In doing this, it is important to be sensitive to the impact that the proposed changes may have. All changes upset the status quo, which creates resistance. New programs impact the leaders of existing programs that they replace. Changes in program format to more effectively reach one adult age segment may make another segment feel threatened in terms of a longstanding comfort zone. The psychology of change implementation is a subject beyond the scope of this book. But a good principle is to try to involve in the implementation process those who are most likely to feel negatively impacted. If they understand the rationale and are asked to have a role in its success, they are much more likely to feel needed and considered a vital part to the intended progress in ministry outreach.

Turning to follow-up activities that have a longer-term perspective, some useful lessons can be learned from the business world. Personal experience in corporate life involved long-range planning.

More specifically, it entailed coordinating development of the company's annual long-range plan. This was at a time when long-range planning was in vogue. Management seminars on the subject were common and virtually every progressive company had a long-range plan. My responsibility was to coordinate the effort; issue instructions to the product divisions concerning planning assumptions, data requirements, formats, and schedules; coordinate the data integration and review process; and other related activities. The process was often referred to as the annual "cattle drive" since it was typically kicked off two months prior to year end when the completed plan was due, and because it involved so many people throughout the company in developing plans and data. Data compiled by the various product divisions was then integrated and reviewed at the corporate level and translated into a composite long-range plan in the form of visual presentations and a very elaborate document.

However, within a few months after it was completed, the long-range plan document would find its way into the bottom desk drawers of the recipients and be virtually forgotten, having become obsolete. Circumstances changed rapidly in this volatile industry. The ten-year forecasts proved to be virtually meaningless when economic conditions changed, unforeseen competitive actions emerged, or rapidly changing technology caused a redirection in product plans. Today, the annual long-range plan has ceased to exist in its prior form in this company. Instead of a long-range plan, an ongoing planning process has taken its place. Long-range plans are a snapshot in time. They soon become obsolete, particularly for companies that operate in a dynamic market or product environment. The ongoing planning process, on the other hand, is a fluid approach that continuously monitors key indicators and adapts business strategies to changing conditions. The same is true for the Ministries Matrix management approach. It will be a waste of time and effort if the evaluation is viewed as a one-shot deal with no ongoing effort. The conclusions and proposed changes will soon be forgotten, events will arise that draw interest into more immediate and pressing problems, and things will soon revert back to normal—normal meaning status quo with a lack of vision for the future.

The initial Ministries Matrix evaluation requires a significant front-end launch effort by the church leadership, as is true for most start-up activities. For such effort to pay off in the days ahead, the Ministries Matrix evaluation needs to make the transition to an ongoing process—the Ministries Matrix process. This ongoing process requires a very modest level of sustaining effort, unlike the start-up activity, and others can carry it out after the leadership council disbands. More specifically, a mechanism needs to be put in place to monitor progress, evaluate performance, and continuously motivate and assure that plans are implemented over time and updated as necessary. If there is no assigned responsibility to do this, the plan developed will become an end in itself. To make this transition to an ongoing process once the leadership council has been disbanded, a Board of Ministries should be established. This board is described more fully in an organizational context in Chapter 9. Its role is to carry out the follow-up Ministries Matrix activities alluded to, as well as other management functions described in Chapters 8 and 9.

Chapter 8

Visibility

In addition to the Ministries Matrix process described in the preceding chapter, other management oversight tools should be considered. One of the most powerful revolves around the simple concept of "visibility"—performance visibility, that is. The Board of Ministries, mentioned in the last chapter and discussed further in this chapter and in Chapter 9, would be the logical focal point to carry on this supervision.

Most medium- and large-sized corporations have what is called a management control room (sometimes a "war room"). It is usually a large room with a conference table, with the walls of the room lined with charts and data that show program status against targets or forecasts, as well as other important statistical data. Its purpose is to provide visibility as to how well the company is performing. Visibility translates into accountability and motivation. The same concept would make a great deal of sense for churches. One of the missing ingredients in church management is visibility regarding performance in terms of effective outreach and fulfillment of defined purposes. The Ministries Matrix process is one element of such visibility. It brings into focus whether the current and planned ministries are the right mix to accomplish goals. But even if the right ministries are in place, the bottom line is how well these ministries are working in terms of the results they are intended to produce. The additional management tool proposed, therefore, is performance visibility. The optimum setting is a room dedicated for this purpose. It might be called the "Ministries Visibility Room." The Ministries Matrix, maintained on an up-to-date basis, would be one of the charts on the wall. Other typical charts might include the following.

EVANGELISM VISIBILITY

- The number of recorded conversions to Christ among children ministries, cumulative plot by quarter, current year
- The number of recorded conversions among youth ministries, cumulative plot by quarter, current year
- The number of recorded conversions among adult ministries, cumulative plot by quarter, current year

GROWTH VISIBILITY

- Worship service attendance, plotted monthly, last year and the current year
- Children Sunday school attendance, plotted monthly, last year and the current year
- Youth Sunday school attendance, plotted monthly, last year and the current year
- Adult Sunday school attendance, plotted monthly, last year and the current year
- Small group ministries attendance, plotted monthly, last year and the current year
- Number of visitors, plotted monthly and cumulatively year-to-date, current year
- Number of visitation calls made, plotted monthly and cumulatively year-to-date, current year

DISCIPLESHIP VISIBILITY

- Enrollment in lay witness classes, plotted for each new class at start-up for the current year
- Number of personal invitations extended to attend a church service program, plotted quarterly and cumulatively year-to-date, current year
- Number of persons counseled, plotted quarterly and cumulatively year-to-date, current year
- Church worker ratio (anyone with a defined role—teacher, usher, board member, youth worker, etc.—as a percent of total membership), plotted quarterly, current year

GENERATIONAL VISIBILITY

- Percentage distribution of worship service attendees by generational category (Youth (ages 13-18), Busters (ages 19-35), Boomers (ages 36-53), Pre-Boomers (ages 54 and above), plotted quarterly, current year

Other charts would evolve over time as information needs were recognized, but those listed above would represent a good start. Much of the data to produce charts of this type could be derived from properly designed attendance registration cards that each attendee would be asked to fill out at each worship service. Other information, such as Christian conversions, visitation calls, class enrollment, persons counseled, etc., would be compiled from records that leaders of each of the appropriate programs or ministries would be asked to maintain. Preparing and maintaining the charts is a ministry opportunity for the right person. If there are engineers, accountants, or business-oriented people in the congregation, they would be ideal candidates. As mentioned, overall responsibility for this "visibility" ministry would fall under the Board of Ministries.

A visibility room of this type would provide a logical setting for church board, Sunday school staff, visitation team, and other leadership meetings. An awareness of performance is an important motivational factor. That is why children get report cards, employees get performance reviews, and executives are often put on incentive plans. It would keep church performance before the church leadership, providing motivation and the basis for focusing on the issues important to the church in fulfilling its mission.

Chapter 9

Organization

Churches can organize in many ways and most of them can be made to work. Sometimes they are built around the personalities and capabilities of people available to take on various responsibilities. This is a valid consideration. But apart from such influences, the tendency is to keep doing things the way they have always been done, leaving well enough alone, and avoiding changes that may disrupt established patterns. This may foster the retention of cumbersome and ineffective organization structures which, though workable, may not provide the optimum utilization of people and resources. As part of the ministries management process, organization structure should also be subject to a critical review. Although innumerable variations are possible concerning the organization of church ministries, just two fundamental concepts are pertinent: functional integration and age integration. All of the possible variations represent some combination of these two basic concepts, which are illustrated conceptually in Exhibit 9.1. The different ministries or groups of related ministries of the church are represented by the numerical designations listed on the left-hand side of each matrix. Only three numbers are listed to display the concept. Obviously, many more programs or functional families would actually exist. The vertical columns of the matrices represent different age categories. Each of the various ministries fits into one or more of these age categories.

ORGANIZATION BY FUNCTION

The top matrix illustrates the "functional integration" organizational concept in which all ministries that belong to the same func-

EXHIBIT 9.1. Organization Concepts

FUNCTIONAL INTEGRATION ORGANIZATION CONCEPT

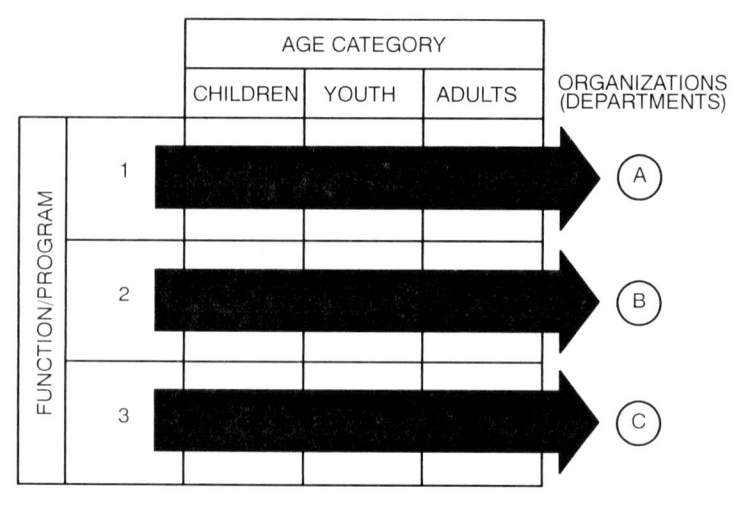

AGE INTEGRATION ORGANIZATION CONCEPT

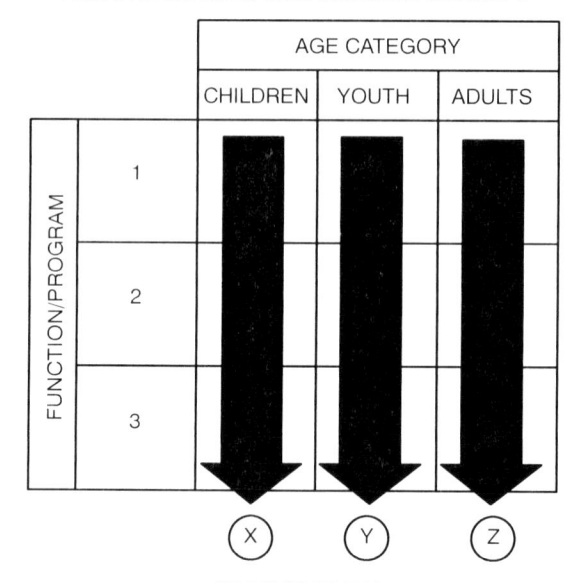

tional family, many of which may extend across several age categories, are placed under a single administrative authority. Using the Sunday school program as an example, the classes for all three age categories ultimately fall under the primary authority of a single administrative focal point—it may be the sunday school superintendent or the Christian education director. Each age category in the Sunday school program would likely be organized under a separate department (e.g., the children's Sunday school, youth Sunday school, and adult Sunday school); nevertheless, the overall administrative line of authority still runs horizontally, as indicated by the upper matrix of Exhibit 9.1; and these departments all fall under the overall administrative jurisdiction of a single Sunday school supervisory authority. The illustration is oversimplified, of course. In reality, the ministries represented by numerical designations on the left-hand side of the matrix would likely be groups of ministries that have strong functional interrelationships. For example, if the Sunday school, the youth activity club program, children's church, home Bible studies, internship programs, vacation Bible school, and the release time program are all considered to be elements of Christian education, they could logically be grouped under this functional family. These programs would all fall under the jurisdiction of the Christian education office or its equivalent under the functional integration concept.

Another functional group might be evangelism, led by a minister or director of evangelism. Programs such as neighborhood child evangelism clubs, special youth outreach ministries, Christian camping programs, institutional ministries (jail services, nursing, and retirement home ministries), coffeehouse ministries, visitation programs, and other evangelism-oriented ministries would fall under the evangelism functional family. Another functional group might be an undershepherding or a family ministries category that would include adult fellowship groups, small group ministries, new member indoctrination and assimilation, and others that have in common the functional theme of building and healing family relationships or care type needs.

ORGANIZATION BY AGE

The other basic concept, "age integration," is illustrated by the lower matrix of Exhibit 9.1. Under this concept, functional considerations are subordinated to age considerations in terms of overall administrative jurisdiction and organizational responsibility. Accordingly, all of the ministries within a given age bracket are organized under a common administrative authority. For example, all of the youth programs would fall under the jurisdiction of a youth director, minister of youth, or perhaps a youth committee. This would include junior and senior high Sunday school, youth activity clubs, youth fellowship groups, youth camping programs, and youth summer programs. Similarly, all ministries or programs that are oriented toward children would fall under the jurisdiction of a children's department, headed by a minister or director of children's ministries. The same idea is true for adult programs or ministries, which would fall under the jurisdiction of a department of adult ministries.

Under the age integration organization structure, a few selected ministries or programs would still remain functionally oriented due to their specialized nature or the fact that they minister to several age levels concurrently. These would typically include the worship service and related activities, music ministries, and counseling programs. It would be impractical to have separate ministries for these functions for each age level.

Exhibits 9.2 and 9.3 illustrate how the same programs and ministries might be organized under each of these two organizational concepts.

The Benefits of Age Integration

The best organization concept is influenced to some degree by church size. Smaller churches with limited personnel may find functional integration to be the only realistic option. However, age integration offers substantial benefits and makes good sense for medium- to large-sized churches (over 200 attendees). Some of the benefits of the age-integrated organization are these:

- Provides the framework for a coordinated and balanced ministry to each age group.
- Makes for more effective scheduling of activities within each age category, avoiding time conflict and overlap
- Avoids the artificial segregation of inseparable functions. For example, the Sunday school is largely oriented toward Christian education but also provides the potential for evangelistic outreach and discipleship training. Organization by age keeps these functions together for each age level under a single authority.
- Since age-level characteristics vary, the programs for each are administered most effectively under the leadership of people who are trained in, knowledgeable about, or who specialize in leading each particular age group.

MINISTRIES OVERSIGHT AND INTERFACE

Ongoing ministries supervision and interface requirements exist under both the functional and age integration organization concepts. Under the functional organization concept, churches typically handle this by reporting the functional families to an associate pastor, a board of Christian education, the senior pastor, or possibly to the church board. Under the age integration concept, similar options might be used, except that age-oriented organizations are involved and a Christian education board would not be applicable. However, none of these options are suitable, assuming use of the Ministries Matrix management process described in earlier chapters. Instead, the ongoing ministries oversight and interface functions should be handled through a Board of Ministries, as mentioned earlier. This would apply under either the functional or age-integrated concepts. The Board of Ministries would carry on the sustaining oversight role after the leadership council has been disbanded. It would monitor progress, evaluate performance, assure that plans are properly implemented over time, and update or revise plans as necessary.

In addition to maintaining the ministries plan on a current basis, the Board of Ministries would serve as the focal point for coordinative interface between the various organizations for which it has oversight responsibility. This would typically include:

- Establishing uniform standards for teachers and leaders
- Approving curriculum and teaching materials to assure doctrinal compatibility with the church position
- Assuring that personnel recruiting and assignments reflect and accommodate the needs of each of the major ministry divisions on an equitable basis
- Planning and allocating space and facilities resources
- Providing other coordination as necessary for functions that cut across age levels (age integration structure), or functional family divisions (functional integration structure)

Exhibits 9.2 and 9.3 illustrate how the Board of Ministries would appear under either organizational concept. While the age integration concept of organization is not new, it has been underemphasized and underutilized. The transition from the functional approach can be implemented on a phased basis as personnel turns over. Smaller churches with limited staff might consider organization by age as a possible pattern to accommodate future staff expansion as growth occurs and makes such expansion possible.

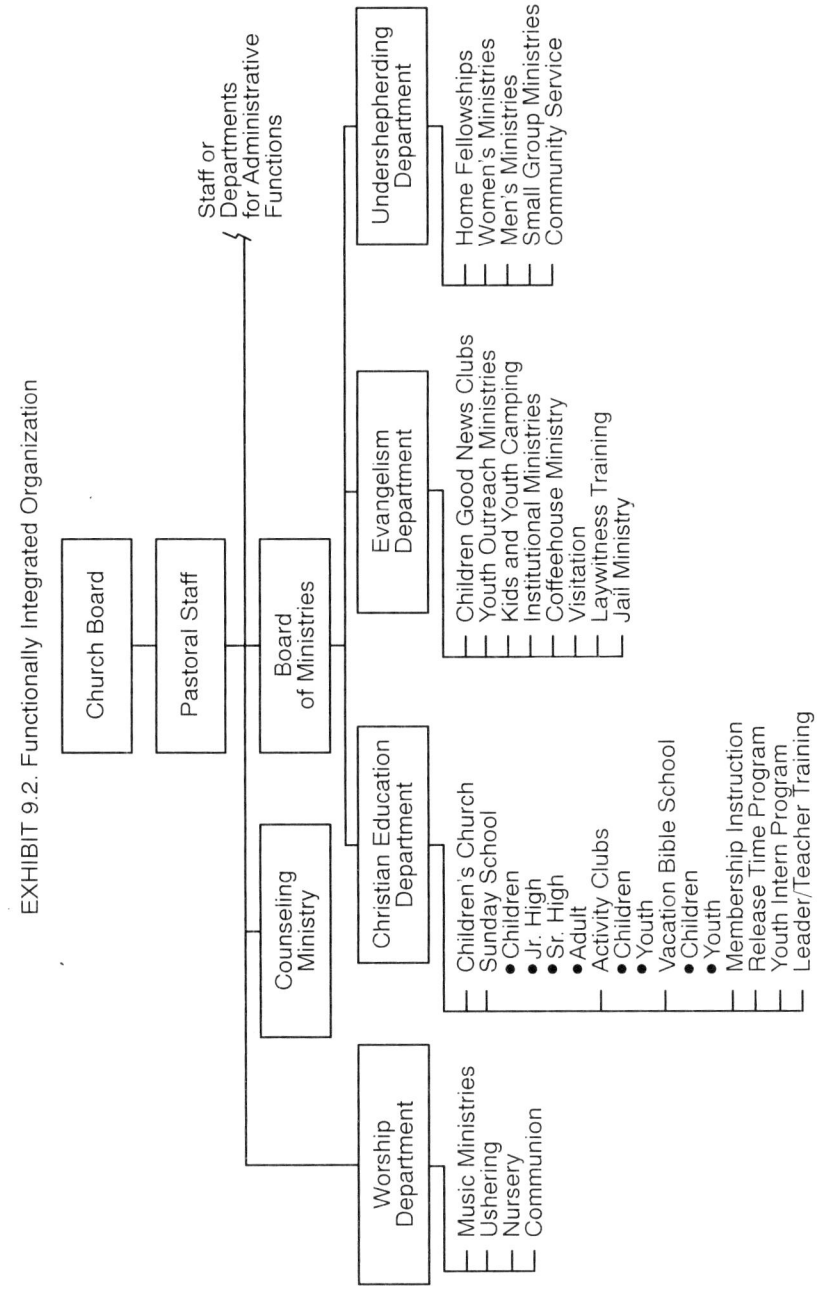

EXHIBIT 9.2. Functionally Integrated Organization

```
                    ┌──────────────┐
                    │ Church Board │
                    └──────┬───────┘
                           │
                    ┌──────┴───────┐
                    │Pastoral Staff│──── Staff or
                    └──────┬───────┘     Departments
                           │              for Administrative
                    ┌──────┴───────┐      Functions
                    │    Board     │
                    │ of Ministries│
                    └──────┬───────┘
                           │
     ┌──────────┬──────────┼──────────────┬──────────────┐
┌────┴─────┐ ┌──┴───────┐ ┌┴────────────┐ ┌┴──────────┐ ┌┴──────────────┐
│ Worship  │ │Counseling│ │  Christian  │ │Evangelism │ │Undershepherding│
│Department│ │ Ministry │ │  Education  │ │Department │ │  Department   │
│          │ │          │ │ Department  │ │           │ │               │
└──────────┘ └──────────┘ └─────────────┘ └───────────┘ └───────────────┘
```

Worship Department
- Music Ministries
- Ushering
- Nursery
- Communion

Christian Education Department
- Children's Church
- Sunday School
  - • Children
  - • Jr. High
  - • Sr. High
  - • Adult
- Activity Clubs
  - • Children
  - • Youth
- Vacation Bible School
  - • Children
  - • Youth
- Membership Instruction
- Release Time Program
- Youth Intern Program
- Leader/Teacher Training

Evangelism Department
- Children Good News Clubs
- Youth Outreach Ministries
- Kids and Youth Camping
- Institutional Ministries
- Coffeehouse Ministry
- Visitation
- Laywitness Training
- Jail Ministry

Undershepherding Department
- Home Fellowships
- Women's Ministries
- Men's Ministries
- Small Group Ministries
- Community Service

121

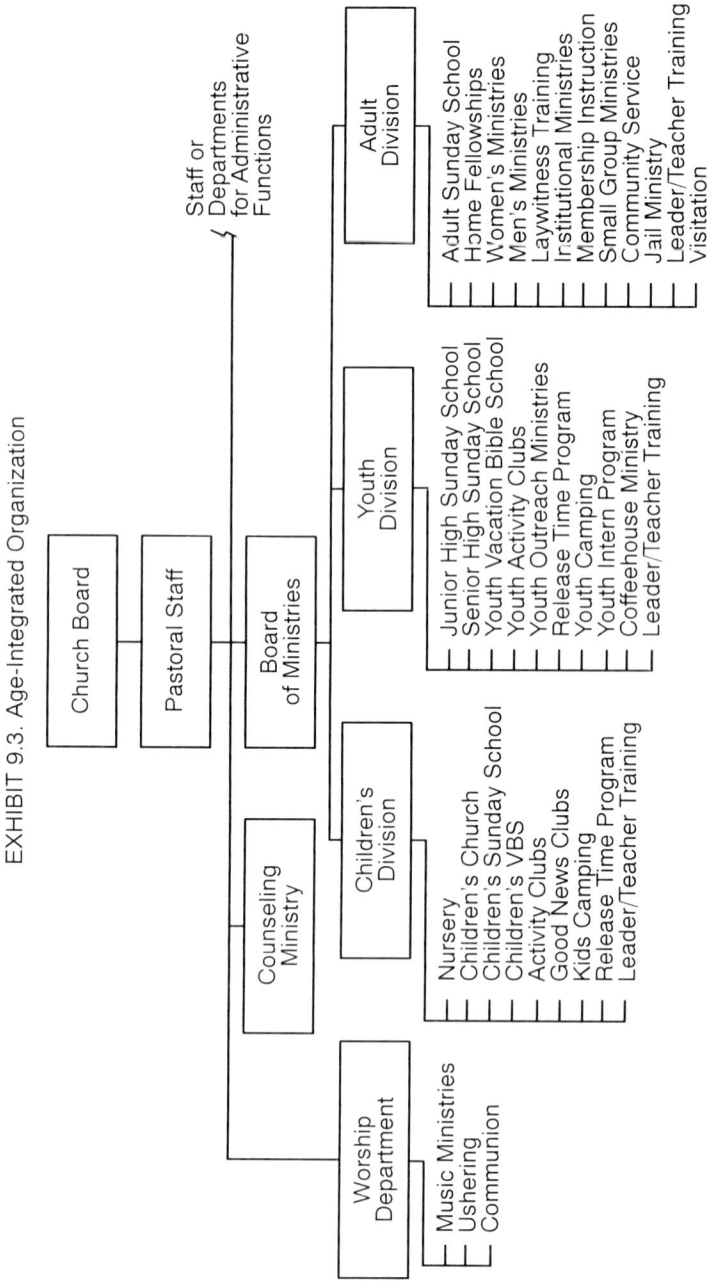

EXHIBIT 9.3. Age-Integrated Organization

```
                          Church Board
                               |
                          Pastoral Staff
                               |
                        Board of Ministries ----- Staff or Departments
                               |                  for Administrative Functions
   ┌──────────┬───────────────┼────────────┬──────────────┐
Worship    Counseling    Children's      Youth          Adult
Department  Ministry     Division       Division       Division
```

Worship Department
- Music Ministries
- Ushering
- Communion

Children's Division
- Nursery
- Children's Church
- Children's Sunday School
- Children's VBS
- Activity Clubs
- Good News Clubs
- Kids Camping
- Release Time Program
- Leader/Teacher Training

Youth Division
- Junior High Sunday School
- Senior High Sunday School
- Youth Vacation Bible School
- Youth Activity Clubs
- Youth Outreach Ministries
- Release Time Program
- Youth Camping
- Youth Intern Program
- Coffeehouse Ministry
- Leader/Teacher Training

Adult Division
- Adult Sunday School
- Home Fellowships
- Women's Ministries
- Men's Ministries
- Laywitness Training
- Institutional Ministries
- Membership Instruction
- Small Group Ministries
- Community Service
- Jail Ministry
- Leader/Teacher Training
- Visitation

122

Chapter 10

The Challenge of Change

The church faces a number of unique challenges today. As stated in an earlier chapter, one of these is the challenge of a largely unevangelized America. Surveys conclude that as many as 60 percent of American adults do not regularly attend church, and an estimated 70 percent are not born-again or evangelical Christians. With an adult population of 200 million, that translates into an unevangelized market of about 140 million American adults. Other surveys put the unchurched figure at a lower percentage, but under all surveys the number remains extremely large.

The market challenge facing the church today is extremely complex. It is more complex than that faced by the commercial world as companies seek to promote their goods and services to consumers. In the commercial world the public creates a demand for consumer products, and companies compete to fulfill that demand. The church, on the other hand, seeks to penetrate a large potential consumer market, much of which is not asking for its services, does not recognize that it has a need for them, and in some cases is outright hostile to the services it offers at no cost. Every individual has a spiritual longing that needs to be satisfied if true fulfillment in life is to be achieved. The church has the answer for many and needs to exploit this reality to its maximum potential.

The present market for the church is both culturally diverse and multigenerational in nature. The multigenerational aspect to ministries management is not new. The church has always ministered to a broad age spectrum. What is new is that the transfer of basic core values and cultural mores from one generation to the next has been largely disrupted. Such core values and cultural attitudes transcended age in an earlier era and provided a certain cultural continuity. That continuity no longer exists, at least not to the degree that it once did. Whatever the reason—economy, politics, media desensitization of immorality, communication, technology, social mobility, internationalization, or other—the successive generations comprising today's market have each undergone uniquely different life experiences that have shaped their attitudes, values, expectations, morality, lifestyles, spiritual perspectives, and aspirations—in short, their respective cultures.

Two basic alternatives exist for the church in meeting the challenge of a culturally diverse multigenerational market. One is to structure the ministries along well-established traditional lines that have worked well in the past, and trust that such an agenda will continue to be effective. The other is to analyze the market in terms of the unique characteristics of the generational components that now comprise it and tailor the ministries accordingly. Unfortunately, most established organizations—companies as well as churches—tend to follow the first approach. Historically, organizations have found it difficult to intentionally introduce new products or services that are likely to create obsolescence or displacement of those that have been at the heart of past success. The manufacturers of horse-drawn carriages were displaced by new companies that introduced horseless carriages (automobiles). Airline companies were composed of newcomers that ultimately displaced railroad companies as the primary players in the passenger transportation industry. The railroads were product oriented rather than transportation oriented in terms of their business vision, mission statement, or basic purpose for existence.

Churches can become ministry-oriented rather than purpose-oriented. Ministries can become an end in themselves, rather than the means to an end. This explains why it is often much more difficult for established churches to reorient current ministries or launch new ones in order to remain relevant in a changing cultural environment than for new churches that adopt a different ministry agenda at the outset. Start-up churches are not burdened with yesterday's ministries' baggage. New churches take root in communities where established churches already exist because spiritual needs are not being met. Established churches tend to become focused on congregational needs (the internal market) and lose their vision for the 70 percent who are either unchurched or unevangelized (the external market).

New churches are typically formed with this vision and motivation, which probably explains the attendance decline experienced by most mainline denominations, while churches that are nondenominational or independent have been the primary area of church growth.

In view of these considerations, the church that seeks to remain relevant in today's environment must be able to respond quickly to change and adopt a much more organized and flexible approach than was typically the case in an earlier era. The church needs to better understand each generational group and how to relate and communicate to them, and to structure innovative ministries that do this effectively. It needs to maintain a purpose-oriented ministries approach and a plan for its implementation. It also needs an accountability system to monitor progress against such a plan. All of this translates into a more formal management discipline. Although the management techniques to do this are relatively simple, their impact can be profound. The real issue is the hurdle of change and the will to initiate such a process. The following are some excerpts from a speech by Dr. J. Don Jennings[1] that aptly sum up the challenge of change today:

> Do we understand that our culture is going through a time of transition? And do we remember that the church went through a period like this before? It too was an age of philosophical relativism and religious pluralism. The climate then too was also one that tolerated sexual perversion, brutal violence and opposition to the truth.
>
> And when was this? This was the Roman Empire at its decline and fall. This was the setting in which the early church successfully evangelized despite conflict and even martyrdom!
>
> Let us not forget that conditions breed opportunity! What an opportunity for the church to be salt and light!
>
> Change is always risky, often painful, and it isn't accomplished by apathetic men and women. It requires high motivation to break through the rigidities of an aging organization.
>
> Although times have changed, many churches continue to be guided by outdated ministry paradigms and all they have to do to go out of business is to stay in business as usual!

As already discussed, two essentials for the church to remain relevant in today's change-prone society are properly defined purposes and interrelated ministries or programs. Emphasis is on the word "interrelated." Unfortunately, churches that go through the discipline of defining purposes often fail in their planning to make the extremely important programming connection. It cannot be overemphasized that purposes without programs that are designed and monitored to fulfill them usually end up as good intentions, never progressing beyond the status of theoretical ideals. In effect, they become purposes with no place to go in terms of implementation. Similarly, programs that are not purpose-oriented are like rudderless ships adrift at sea. They tend to become an end in themselves, rather than a means to an end—namely, the reasons for which the church exists. Accordingly, interrelating purposes and programs through the type of systematic approach outlined in previous chapters, and in the context of today's generation-based cultural diversity, is offered as the paramount guiding principle for achieving dynamic church growth and outreach during this decade of ongoing change.

Notes

Chapter 1

1. George Barna, *Evangelism That Works* (Ventura, CA: Regal Books, 1995), pp. 38, 53.

Chapter 2

1. *Statistical Abstract of the United States: 1998 (118th Edition)*, Table No. 16. Resident Population by Sex and Age: 1997 (Washington, DC: U.S. Census Bureau, 1998), p. 16.
2. Ken Dychtwald and Joe Flower, *Age Wave* (Los Angeles, CA: Jeremy P. Tarcher, Inc., 1989), pp. 13-21.
3. James Bell, *Bridge Over Troubled Water* (Colorado Springs, CO: Cook Communications Ministries, Chariot Victor Publishing, 1993), p. 31. Used by permission. May not be further reproduced. All rights reserved.
4. Leith Anderson, *Dying for Change* (Minneapolis, MN: Bethany House Publishers, 1990), pp. 75-99.
5. Ibid., p. 95.
6. William Easum, *How to Reach Baby Boomers* (Nashville, TN: Abingdon Press, 1991), pp. 73-92.
7. Jimmy Long, *Generating Hope: A Strategy for Reaching the Postmodern Generation* (Downers Grove, IL: Inter-Varsity Press, 1997), pp. 36-54.
8. Ibid., p. 156.
9. George Barna, *Evangelism That Works* (Ventura, CA: Regal Books, 1995), p. 112. Used by permission.
10. George Barna, *Generation Next* (Ventura, CA: Regal Books, 1995), p. 11.
11. Ibid., p. 118. Used by permission.
12. *Statistical Abstract of the United States: 1998 (118th Edition)*, Table No. 17, Resident Population Projections by Age and Sex: 1998 to 2050, (Washington, DC: U.S. Census Bureau, 1998), p. 17.
13. Sara Rimer, "Older People Want to Work in Retirement, Survey Finds," *The New York Times*, Thursday, September 2, 1999; p. A10.
14. Woodrow Kroll, *The Vanishing Ministry* (Grand Rapids, MI: Kregal Publications, 1991), p. 132. Used by permission.
15. J. Don Jennings, <WWW.TIMEOUT!.COM>, 68th Annual Conference of the General Association of Regular Baptist Churches, Keynote Address, June 26, 1999.

16. Leith Anderson, *A Church for the 21st Century* (Minneapolis, MN: Bethany House Publishers, 1992), pp. 143-161; Jimmy Long, *Generating Hope: A Strategy for Reaching the Postmodern Generation* (Downers Grove, IL: InterVarsity Press, 1997), pp. 158-211.

Chapter 3

1. William Benke and Milt Bryan, "The World's Most Fruitful Field," *Evangelizing Today's Child,* 14(6), November/December, 1977 (pp. 4-6, 44-45), (Warrenton, MO: Child Evangelism Fellowship, Inc.). Used by permission.
2. George Barna, *Generation Next* (Ventura, CA: Regal Books, 1995), pp. 77-79. Used by permission.
3. J. Irvin Overholtzer, "Child Evangelism As Taught in the Word of God." In *The Indomitable Mr. O,* Norman Rohrer (Ed.), (pp. 146-153), (Warrenton, MO: Child Evangelism Fellowship Press, 1970).
4. Benke and Bryan, "The World's Most Fruitful Field," p. 44.
5. George Barna, *Generation Next,* p. 77.
6. Roy B. Zuck and Gene A. Getz, *Christian Youth: An In-Depth Study* (Chicago, IL: Moody Press, 1968).
7. "Gallup: U.S. Religious Attitudes Similar to Those of 1947," *Presbyterian News Service,* May 20, 1997. <http://www.ecunet.org/pcnews/oldnews/1997/97208.htm>
8. George Barna, *The Index of Leading Spiritual Indicators* (Nashville, TN: Word Publishing, 1996), pp. 1-5.
9. Elmer L. Towns, "Evangelism: The Why and How." In *Church Growth State of the Art,* C. Peter Wagner (Ed.), (p. 53), (Wheaton, IL: Tyndale House Publishers, Inc., 1986).
10. George H. Gallup Jr., "Six Basic Spiritual Needs of Americans." In *Yearbook of American and Canadian Churches 1992,* Kenneth Bedell and Alice M. Jones (Eds.), (p. 15), (Nashville, TN: Abingdon Press, 1992).
11. Ibid., pp. 15-16.
12. Bill Hull, *7 Steps to Transform Your Church* (Grand Rapids, MI: Fleming H. Revell, 1993), pp. 167-171.
13. Ibid., p. 161.
14. Ibid., p. 162; James F. Engel, "Who's Really Doing Evangelism?", *Christianity Today,* December 16, 1991 (pp. 35-37).
15. Bill Hull, *7 Steps to Transform Your Church,* p. 167.
16. Ken Hemphill and R. Wayne Jones, *Growing an Evangelistic Sunday School* (Nashville, TN: Broadman Press, 1989), pp. 97-125.
17. George Barna, *The Second Coming of the Church* (Nashville, TN: Word Publishing, 1998), pp. 15-17; Woodrow Kroll, *The Vanishing Ministry* (Grand Rapids, MI: Kregal Publications, 1991), pp. 31-33; Leith Anderson, *Dying for Change* (Minneapolis, MN: Bethany House Publishers, 1990), pp. 50-51; George Barna, *The Index of Leading Spiritual Indicators* (Dallas, TX: Word Publishing, 1996), p. 109.

18. *Yearbook of American and Canadian Churches 2000*, 68th Issue, Eileen W. Lindner (Ed.), Table 1, Inclusive Membership 1890-1998. (Nashville, TN: Abingdon Press), p. 10.

19. Charles W. Wolson, *The Body* (Nashville, TN: Word Publishing, 1992), p. 345; *PRRC Emerging Trends* (May 1991):1 <http://www.sermon.illustrations.com/newpage332.ntm>

20. George Barna, *Evangelism That Works* (Ventura, CA: Regal Books, 1995), pp. 47, 54-56.

21. *Community Impact Bulletins*, Washington Family Council, PO Box 40584, Bellevue, WA 98015.

22. Larry Burkett, *The Complete Financial Guide for Single Parents* (Colorado Springs, CO: Victor Chariot Publishing, 1992).

Chapter 5

1. Alvin J. Lindgren and Norman Shawchuck, *Management for Your Church* (Nashville, TN: Abingdon Press, 1977), pp. 46-47. Reprinted 1984, Leith, ND: Spiritual Growth Resources, a division of Organizational Resources Press, Ltd.

2. Jimmy Long, *Generating Hope: A Strategy for Reaching the Postmodern Generation* (Downers Grove, IL: Inter-Varsity Press, 1997), pp. 19-35.

Chapter 7

1. Rick Warren, *The Purpose-Driven Church* (Grand Rapids, MI: Zondervan Publishing House, 1995), p. 146.

Chapter 10

1. J. Don Jennings, <WWW.TIMEOUT!.COM> 68th Annual Conference of the General Association of Regular Baptist Churches, Keynote Address, June 26, 1999.

Recommended Reading

Anderson, Leith (1990). *Dying for Change*. Minneapolis, MN: Bethany House Publishers.
Anderson, Leith (1992). *A Church for the 21st Century*. Minneapolis, MN: Bethany House Publishers.
Barna, George (1995). *Evangelism That Works*. Ventura, CA: Regal Books.
Barna, George (1995). *Generation Next*. Ventura, CA: Regal Books.
Barna, George (1996). *The Index of Leading Spiritual Indicators*. Nashville, TN: Word Publishing.
Barna, George (1998). *The Second Coming of the Church*. Nashville, TN: Word Publishing.
Hemphill, Ken and R. Wayne Jones (1989). *Growing an Evangelistic Sunday School*. Nashville, TN: Broadman Press.
Kroll, Woodrow (1991). *The Vanishing Ministry*. Grand Rapids, MI: Kregal Publications.
Long, Jimmy (1997). *Generating Hope: A Strategy for Reaching the Postmodern Generation*. Downers Grove, IL: Inter-Varsity Press.
Rohrer, Norman, Ed. (1970). *The Indomitable Mr. O*. Warrenton, MO: Child Evangelism Fellowship Press.
Warren, Rick (1995). *The Purpose-Driven Church*. Grand Rapids, MI: Zondervan Publishing House.

Ministries Matrix

WHAT \ TO WHOM	PURPOSES OF THE LOCAL CHURCH				
	CHILDREN (Under age 12)	YOUTH (Ages 13-18)	ADULTS		
			GENERATION X (Baby Busters)	BABY BOOMERS	PRE-BOOMERS
	1	6	11	16	21
	2	7	12	17	22
	3	8	13	18	23
	4	9	14	19	24
	5	10	15	20	25

Listing of Current Ministries

AGE CATEGORY	CURRENT PROGRAM	PURPOSE CATEGORY		PROGRAM EFFECTIVENESS			
		PRIMARY	SECONDARY	CHILDREN OR YOUTH	GEN. X	ADULTS BABY BOOMERS	PRE-BOOMERS

Index

Page numbers followed by the letter "e" indicate an exhibit.

Abortion, 20
Action-oriented purpose, 68
Administrative functions, 2
Adult discipleship ministries, 44
Adult evangelism, 42-46
Age gradation, 74
Age grouping, 27
Age integration, 116e, 118-119, 122e
Age Wave, 11
Alcoholism, 21
Allegheny Center Alliance Church (Pittsburgh, PA), 51
American Family Association, 55
Anderson, Leith, 14-16, 17
Assimilating church, 68, 69, 70
Attendance, church, 6, 7e
Authority, ignoring, 20

Baby Boomers, 5, 9, 10e, 10, 11-19
    population distribution, 11e
Baby Busters. *See* Generation X
Barna, George
    on adult evangelism, 43
    on child evangelism, 34
    on the family, 29
    on Generation X, 22
    on the unchurched, 49
    on Youth, 24, 40
Battling church, 68, 69, 70
Bell, James, 14
Belmont Church (Nashville, TN), 49
Belonging, sense of, 72
Bible clubs, weekday, 38

Bible study, 31e
Biblical passages
    Acts 6, 62
    Ephesians 4, 7
    Exodus 18, 61-62
    Joshua 14, 27
    Matthew 18, 36
    Matthew 22, 68
    Matthew 28, 61, 68
    Proverbs 16, 62
    Proverbs 18, 62
    Proverbs 24, 62
    Proverbs 29, 66
    Romans 12, 73
Big Brother/Big Sister ministries, 27, 39, 50, 56
Billy Graham Crusades, 34-35
Birth rate, 13e
Blazers, 9, 10e, 10, 11e, 24-25
Board of Ministries, 109, 111, 113, 119
ten Boom, Corrie, 36
Boomer Ministries, 30e-31e, 95e
"Bottom-line" mentality, 3-4
Bridge Over Troubled Water, 14
Builders, 9, 10e, 11e, 24-25
Building Committee, 1
Burkett, Larry, 50

Campelo, Tony, 56
Car Care Saturday, 49-50
Celebration (worship), 68
Cell groups, 22

135

Change
  challenge of, 123-136
  comfort with, 15
Child evangelism, 33-39
"Child Evangelism As Taught in the Word of God," 35
Child Evangelism Fellowship (CEF), 33-34, 35, 37
  Good News Club, 36, 38, 72, 104
Children, 9, 10
Children Ministries, 94e
Christ Temple Church (Meridian, MI), 55
Christian Coalition, 69
Christian culturism, 43
Christian education. *See* Religious education; Sunday school
Christian Service Brigade, 38
"Christian Youth: An In-Depth Study," 40
Christianity Today, 44-45
Church loyalty, 30e
Church ministries, 2. *See also individual listings*
Church selection, 41
Church size, 46-48
Churches
  Allegheny Center Alliance Church (Pittsburgh, PA), 51
  Belmont Church (Nashville, TN), 49
  Christ Temple Church (Meridian, MI), 55
  City Foursquare Church (Seattle, WA), 51
  First Baptist Church (Bellevue, WA), 26
  Grace Church. *See* Grace Church
  Overlake Christian Church (Redmond, WA), 39, 66, 102
  Plymouth Brethren (DeWitt, MI), 52
  Real Life Church (Maple Valley, WA), 101

Churches *(continued)*
  Richland Baptist Church (Richland, WA), 57
  University Presbyterian Church (Seattle, WA), 103
  Wenatchee Free Methodist Church (Wenatchee, WA), 54
  Woodside New Life Assembly of God (Marysville, WA), 51
  City Foursquare Church (Seattle, WA), 51
Coding, Ministries Matrix, 85-86
College age, boomers, 12
Community Impact Bulletin, 49
"Community Outreach and Service," 70, 73e, 94e-95e, 105. *See also* Ministries Matrix
Community renewal, 54
Community service, 48-57
Compatible, 59, 60e
Complete Financial Guide for Single Parents, The, 50
Confidence, and evangelism, 45
Contemporary evening worship service, 104
Conventional Christianity, 101
Conversion
  in adulthood, 42, 43
  age at, 34
  parent as factor in, 40-41
Coalition for Community Renewal (CCR), 54
Community Impact Committee, 57
Counseling, 72
Crisis ministries, 19
Cultural war, 69
Current programming, recording, 86, 88e, 89-91, 133

Deacon Skeptic, 84-85
Denver Seminary, 44
"Depth Study" technique, 81
Dial-a-children's story, 17
Direct evangelism, 71-72

Direct purpose, 67
Discipleship, 73e, 90, 94e-95e. *See also* Ministries Matrix
Discipleship Visibility, 112
Diversity, tolerance for, 15
Divorce, 20, 23
Dobson, James, 36
"Donnybrooks," 71
Door hanger literature, 101
Dresser Ministry, 52
Dychtwald, Ken, 11
Dying for Change, 14-16

Edwards, Jonathan, 36
Emerald City Outreach Ministries, 53
Emotional support, 72
Evaluation, 90
Evangelism. *See also* Child Evangelism Fellowship (CEF); Ministries Matrix
  adult, 42-46
  child, 33-39
  direct, 71-72
  fear and, 45
  friendship, 45
  Grace Church, 94e-95e
  and ministry implications, 31e
  and purpose, 73e
  youth, 40-42
Evangelism That Works, 22
Evangelism visibility, 112
Expectation, high, 15
"Extended family" setting, 103
External markets, 100, 124

Family, spiritual commitment of, 28-29
Family Issues Committee, 54
Family Life Seminars, 52
Family Research Council, 69
Fear, and evangelism, 45
Financial help, 72

"Find yourself," 25
First Baptist Church (Bellevue, WA), 26
Five-Day Clubs, 38
Flock ministry, 26-27
Flower, Joe, 11
Focus on the Family, 36, 42, 69
Focus on the Family, 52
Follow-up activities, 107-109
Food distribution program, 62
Ford, Leighton, 36
Fossil, Elder, 82
Foster care program, 53-54
Friendship evangelism, 45, 72
"Full-service" churches, 16-17
Function, organization by, 115, 117
Functional integration, 115, 116e, 121e

Generating Hope: A Strategy for Reaching the Postmodern Generation, 19, 68
Generation Next, 34
Generation X, 5, 9, 10e, 10, 11e, 19-22
Generation X Ministries, 30e-31e, 94e-95e
Generational categories, 9, 10e. *See also* Baby Boomers; Generation X; Pre-Boomers; Youth
Generational multiculturalism, 5
Generational visibility, 113
Getz, Gene A., 40, 42
Good News Club, 36, 38, 72, 104
"Good Samaritan" lesson, 37
Grace Church, 86, 88e
  Leadership Council, 94e-95e
  Ministries Matrix, 87e, 91, 92e, 93, 96e, 105, 106e, 134
  strategy, 104-105, 106e
Great Commandment, 68
Great Commission, 61, 68
Group studies, 29

Growing an Evangelistic Sunday School, 46
Growth groups, 99
Growth visibility, 112

Habitat for Humanity, 18
Heck, Doug, 51
Hemphill, Ken, 46
Henry, Matthew, 36
High-tech opportunity, 18
Hope for the Children, 53-54
House church, 29-30
   strategy, 102-103
"How To" seminars, 18
Hull, Bill, 44, 45
Human Life Sunday, 55

Implementation, planned, 59, 60e
Index of Leading Spiritual Indicators, The, 43
Independence vs. interdependence, 72, 84
Infancy stage, 11-12
Influencing church, 68, 69, 70
Institute for Church Development, 44
Interface, 119-120
Ironside, Harry A., 38
Intergenerational balance, 81
Internal market (congregation), 100, 124
Interrelated ministries, 126

Jennings, J. Don, 28, 125
Jones, R. Wayne, 46

Kemp, Jeff, 49

"L and D" club, 36
LaHaye, Tim, 52
Latchkey kids, 20
Leadership, 16
Leadership council, 81

Leadership training, 41-42
Life Chain, 54, 57
The Lighthouse, 51
Live-to-work, boomers, 13
Long, Jimmy, 19, 21-22, 68
Loyalty, low, 15

Mack, Michael C., 29
Management, 59-63
Management seminars, 108
Maturity, 74
McNitt, Ann, 52
Meaning seeking, 16
Mears, Henrietta, 36
Medical care ministry, 51
Ministries Matrix, 46, 133e
   coding, 85-86
   current programming
     evaluation of, 91, 93, 134
     recording, 86, 89-91, 133
   Grace Church, 87e, 91, 92e, 93, 96e, 105, 106e, 134
   leadership council, 81
   organizing a, 79-81
   prioritizing, 82-86
   and purpose, 75, 76e, 77
"Ministries Visibility Room," 111
Ministry implications, 28-30, 30e-31e
"Ministry ruts," 4
Ministry-oriented vs. purpose-oriented, 124
"Mission categories," 59, 75, 86
Mission projects, local, 18, 28
Mission statement, 66
Moms-in-Touch, 55
Motivation, 16
Moynihan, Daniel Patrick, 56
Multiculturalism, 5
Multigenerational centralized strategy, 97-98
"Mutual Support and Encouragement," 70, 72, 73e, 94e-95e. *See also* Ministries Matrix

National Day of Prayer Mayor's
    Breakfast Committee, 55
Networking, 29
Nevers, the seven, 66
New horizon purpose categories, 84
Newcomer, needs of, 44
"No priority," 86
Nonaffiliation, 15
Northwest Leadership Foundation, 54

Objectives
    defined, 67
    revisions to, 59
Organization
    by age, 118-119, 121e, 122e
    concepts, 116e
    by function, 115, 117
Overholtzer, J.I., 35, 38. *See also*
    Child Evangelism Fellowship
    (CEF)
Overlake Christian Church
    (Redmond, WA), 39, 66, 102
Oversight, 119-120

Pagliacci Pizza, 51
Parenting workshops, 52-53
Parents' night out, 17
Participatory ministries, 28
Peter D. Hart Research Associates, 25
Petty, Elder, 71
Pieces to Peace Ministry, 39
Pioneer Ministries, 38
Planned implementation, 59, 60e
Plymouth Brethren (DeWitt, MI), 52
Politics, 21
Polycarp, 36
Population, change in by age, 12e
Post Generation X, 11e
Prayer ministries, churchwide, 19
Pre-Boomer Ministries, 30e-31e, 95e
Pre-Boomers, 9, 10, 24-28
Prioritizing, 82-86
Proactive approach, 2, 6

Pro-family issues, 57
Program objectives, 67
Programming imbalances,
    identifying, 59, 60e
Protecting church, 68, 69, 70
Public affairs, community
    involvement in, 56-57
Purpose, 65-75
    defining, 59, 60e
    interrelationship of, 73e
Purpose categories, 89
Purpose-Driven Church, The, 67, 99
Purpose-oriented management, 67.
    See also Purpose

Qualitative ratings, 89

Rainier Valley workshops, 53
Reactive approach, 2, 6
Real Life Church (Maple Valley,
    WA), 101
Refugees, support for, 50
Relationships, weaker, 15
Religious education, at home, 18.
    See also Sunday school
Remedial reading program, 52
Results-oriented, boomers, 13
Retreats, 19
Richland Baptist Church (Richland,
    WA), 57
Rood, Paul W., 38

Saddleback Seminars, 67
Satellite churches, 100-102
School age, boomers, 12
Scope of ministries, 30e
Scripture, 61
Seeker groups, 99
Self-reliance, 23
Sermons, 31e
Service groups, 99
Seven Baskets, 50
7 Steps To Transform Your Church,
    44

Sex, 21
"Shelving" seniors, 26
Short-term vs. long-term perspectives, 85
Silva Mind Control, 13
Single-parent homes, 39, 49-50, 55-56
Single-parent parking, 18
Sit-and-soak worship services, 29
Size, church, 46-48
Small group ministries, 18, 31e
Small group seeker, 105
Small groups strategy, 99-102
Social consciousness, 20
Social gatherings, 72
"Sociopolitical Influence on Moral Issues," 70
Solomon (King), 62
Special Delivery, 50
Special-need support groups, 100
Sport ministries, 18
Stewardship, 31e, 61
Strategy
  follow-up activities to, 107-109
  Grace Church, 104-105, 106e
  house church, 102-103
  multigenerational centralized, 97-98
  satellite churches, 100-102
  small groups, 99-102
  targeted centralized, 98-99
  traditional and contemporary services, 103
Stress, 21, 23
Suicide, 21
Sunday school, 45. *See also* Religious education
  as evangelistic outreach, 72
  and Grace Church strategy, 105
  and house church strategy, 102
  intergenerational membership, 26
  and ministry implications, 31e
  quarterly teachers, 19
  reorientation of, 46

Support groups, 99
  special-need, 100
Synergy Church, The, 29

Targeted centralized strategy, 98-99
Team ministries, 29
Teenagers, 12, 23
Thiessen, Henry C., 38
Traditional and contemporary service strategy, 103
Transcendental Meditation, 13
Transitional ministries, 18
Tri-City Pregnancy Center, 57
Trumbull, Charles G., 38
Trust, 20
Truth, rejection of, 23

Unchanging church, 68, 69, 70
Unchurched, 38, 48, 49, 100, 124
Union Gospel Mission, 53
University Presbyterian Church (Seattle, WA), 103

Vacation with a Purpose, 18
Valley Street House, 51
Visibility, 111-113
Voter Registration Sundays, 54

Walk for Jesus, 57
Warren, Rick, 67, 99
Washington Consultation for United Prayer (W-CUP), 57
Washington Family Council, 49
Watt, Isaac, 36
Weekday ministries, 18
Wenatchee Free Methodist Church (Wenatchee, WA), 54
What Can I Do?, 55
WIFM (what's in it for me), 14
Widows, 27-28, 49

Wilson, Walter L., 38
Women's ministry, 18
Woodside New Life Assembly of
 God (Marysville, WA), 51
Work-to-live, Generation X, 19
World Relief, 50
Worship, 68, 94e-95e. *See also*
 Ministries Matrix
  format, 30e
  and purpose, 73e

Youth, 9, 22-24
Youth Center, 105
Youth evangelism, 40-42
Youth for Christ, 52-53
Youth leaders, 41-42
Youth Ministries, 94e
"Yuppies," 13

Zinzedorf (Count), 36
Zuck, Roy B., 40, 42

Order Your Own Copy of This Important Book for Your Personal Library!

CHURCH WAKE-UP CALL
A Ministries Management Approach That Is Purpose-Oriented and Inter-Generational in Outreach

_____ in hardbound at $49.95 (ISBN: 0-7890-1137-9)

_____ in softbound at $19.95 (ISBN: 0-7890-1138-7)

COST OF BOOKS_____	☐ **BILL ME LATER:** ($5 service charge will be added) (Bill-me option is good on US/Canada/Mexico orders only; not good to jobbers, wholesalers, or subscription agencies.)
OUTSIDE USA/CANADA/ MEXICO: ADD 20%_____	
POSTAGE & HANDLING_____ (US: $4.00 for first book & $1.50 for each additional book Outside US: $5.00 for first book & $2.00 for each additional book)	☐ Check here if billing address is different from shipping address and attach purchase order and billing address information.
	Signature_____
SUBTOTAL_____	☐ **PAYMENT ENCLOSED:** $_____
IN CANADA: ADD 7% GST_____	☐ **PLEASE CHARGE TO MY CREDIT CARD.**
STATE TAX_____ (NY, OH & MN residents, please add appropriate local sales tax)	☐ Visa ☐ MasterCard ☐ AmEx ☐ Discover ☐ Diner's Club ☐ Eurocard ☐ JCB
	Account #_____
FINAL TOTAL_____ (If paying in Canadian funds, convert using the current exchange rate. UNESCO coupons welcome.)	Exp. Date_____
	Signature_____

Prices in US dollars and subject to change without notice.

NAME_____
INSTITUTION_____
ADDRESS_____
CITY_____
STATE/ZIP_____
COUNTRY_____ COUNTY (NY residents only)_____
TEL_____ FAX_____
E-MAIL_____

May we use your e-mail address for confirmations and other types of information? ☐ Yes ☐ No
We appreciate receiving your e-mail address and fax number. Haworth would like to e-mail or fax special discount offers to you, as a preferred customer. **We will never share, rent, or exchange your e-mail address or fax number.** We regard such actions as an invasion of your privacy.

Order From Your Local Bookstore or Directly From
The Haworth Press, Inc.
10 Alice Street, Binghamton, New York 13904-1580 • USA
TELEPHONE: 1-800-HAWORTH (1-800-429-6784) / Outside US/Canada: (607) 722-5857
FAX: 1-800-895-0582 / Outside US/Canada: (607) 772-6362
E-mail: getinfo@haworthpressinc.com
PLEASE PHOTOCOPY THIS FORM FOR YOUR PERSONAL USE.
www.HaworthPress.com

BOF00

Increase your business with the marketing strategies suggested in the following books!

Take 20% Off Each Book! Special Sale

A step-by-step guide to create a biblically based blueprint for your church or ministry!

CHURCH AND MINISTRY STRATEGIC PLANNING
From Concept to Success

R. Henry Migliore, PhD, Robert E. Stevens, PhD, and David L. Loudon, PhD

"The shade of liberalism and conservatism of a given church is not critical to the argument in this book, nor is the theological alignment: It is the church as a service organization that is being addressed."
—Journal of Religion and Psychical Research

$59.95 hard. ISBN: 1-56024-346-5.
Text price (5+ copies): $24.95. 1994. 161 pp. with Index.

Discover specific strategies that will help your athletic department attract fans, increase revenues, and meet goals!

STRATEGIC PLANNING FOR COLLEGIATE ATHLETICS

Deborah A. Yow, PhD, DHum, R. Henry Migliore, PhD, William W. Bowden, EdD, PhD, Robert E. Stevens, PhD, and David L. Loudon, PhD, MBA

Comprehensive and concise, **Strategic Planning for Collegiate Athletics** offers a step-by-step approach to planning and managing successful athletic programs. For athletic administrators at the collegiate level (and those in high school or recreational programs), this valuable resource will help you analyze your organization's environment, set objectives, decide on specific actions, and obtain feedback to create a dynamic plan for your department. Addressing the advantages of devising a blueprint for your athletic enterprise—such as knowing what to expect of colleagues and having a clear picture of future directions—**Strategic Planning for Collegiate Athletics** offers you easily implemented methods and suggestions to help your athletic department develop a map toward greater success and achievement.

$39.95 hard. ISBN: 0-7890-0889-0.
$24.95 soft. ISBN: 0-7890-1057-7.
2000. Available now. 174 pp. with Index.

FACULTY: ORDER YOUR NO-RISK EXAM COPY TODAY! Send us your examination copy order on your stationery; indicate course title, enrollment, and course start date. We will ship and bill on a 60-day examination basis, and cancel your invoice if you decide to adopt! We will always bill at the lowest available price, such as our special "5+ text price." Please remember to order softcover where available. (We cannot provide examination copies of books not published by The Haworth Press, Inc., or its imprints.) (Outside US/Canada, a proforma invoice will be sent upon receipt of your request and must be paid in advance of shipping. A full refund will be issued with proof of adoption.)

Learn to produce an annual report for your nonprofit agency!

USING PUBLIC RELATIONS STRATEGIES TO PROMOTE YOUR NONPROFIT ORGANIZATION

NOW AVAILABLE IN PAPERBACK! Over 200 Pages!

Ruth Ellen Kinzey, MA

Explore an easy-to-follow explanation on why nonprofits must take a more business-like approach in their communications. You will discover instructions on how to make newsletters, annual reports, speakers' bureaus, and board selection easy yet effective.

$59.95 hard. ISBN: 0-7890-0257-4. 1999.
$24.95 soft. ISBN: 0-7890-0258-2. 2000. Available now.
233 pp. with Index.

Discover cross-cultural and cross-disiplinary approaches to marketing issues as seen by marketing academics from around the world!

NEWER INSIGHTS INTO MARKETING
Cross-Cultural and Cross-National Perspectives

Edited by Camille P. Schuster and Phil Harris

Contains case studies, tables, charts, and evaluations of specific marketing campaigns, this book allows marketers and market researchers to learn from the achievements and mistakes of other international companies.

(A monograph published simultaneously as the Journal of Euromarketing, Vol. 7, No. 2.)
$39.95 hard. ISBN: 0-7890-0752-5.
Text price (5+ copies): $19.95. 1999. 94 pp. with Index.

Discover innovative research on attracting, training, and retaining volunteers!

VOLUNTEERISM MARKETING
New Vistas for Nonprofit and Public Sector Management

Edited by Donald R. Self, DBA, and Walter W. Wymer, Jr., DBA

Explores the differing personality traits and characteristics of volunteers in differing fields. This valuable book also contains a systematically arranged section of 131 of the most important research studies on volunteerism.

(A monograph published simultaneously as the Journal of Nonprofit & Public Sector Marketing, Vol. 6, No. 2/3.)
$59.95 hard. ISBN: 0-7890-0967-6.
$39.95 soft. ISBN: 0-7890-0985-4. 1999. 174 pp. with Index.

Best Business Books
An imprint of The Haworth Press, Inc.
10 Alice Street
Binghamton, New York 13904–1580 USA

WE'RE ONLINE!
http://www.HaworthPress.com

Learn how to define and redefine markets to make your company competitive in today's fast-changing global markets!

DEFINING YOUR MARKET
Winning Strategies for High-Tech, Industrial, and Service Firms
Art Weinstein, PhD

"THIS PRACTICAL AND COMPREHENSIVE HOW-TO GUIDE contains research, case studies and a review of the literature on market definition."
—*Educational Book Review*

$59.95 hard. ISBN: 0-7890-0251-5.
$29.95 soft. ISBN: 0-7890-0252-3. 1998. 200 pp. with Index.
Features case studies, tables/figures, review questions, and appendixes.

Named one of Choice's prestigious 34th Annual Outstanding Academic Books list!

THE MARKETING RESEARCH GUIDE
Robert E. Stevens, PhD, Bruce Wrenn, PhD, Morris E. Ruddick, MS, Philip K. Sherwood, EdD

"A fine resource for quickly finding answers to specific questions relating to the application and development of various marketing research techniques."
—*Choice*

Over 450 Pages!

$89.95 hard. ISBN: 1-56024-339-2. 1997.
488 pp. with Index.
Includes a 150-page Instructor's Manual with a test bank and transparency masters.

Learn how effective marketing research can solve a wide spectrum of marketing problems!

MARKETING RESEARCH THAT PAYS OFF
Case Histories of Marketing Research Leading to Success in the Marketplace
Edited by Larry Percy

Over 250 Pages!

This book offers you insight into how actual companies have used market research to successfully solve marketing problems.
$49.95 hard. ISBN: 1-56024-949-8.
$24.95 soft. ISBN: 0-7890-0197-7.
1997. 270 pp. with Index.

NOW AVAILABLE IN PAPERBACK!

MARKETING PLANNING GUIDE, SECOND EDITION
Robert E. Stevens, PhD, Bruce Wrenn, PhD, David L. Loudon, PhD, and William E. Warren, DBA

Over 300 Pages!

$69.95 hard. ISBN: 0-7890-0112-8.
$39.95 soft. ISBN: 0-7890-0241-8 1997. 343 pp. with Index.
Includes a 150-page Instructor's Manual with a test bank and over 175 transparency masters, which feature charts, figures, worksheets, and a bibliography.

CALL OUR TOLL-FREE NUMBER: 1-800-HAWORTH
US & Canada only / 8am-5pm ET; Monday-Friday
Outside US/Canada: + 607-722-5857

FAX YOUR ORDER TO US: 1-800-895-0582
Outside US/Canada: + 607-771-0012

E-MAIL YOUR ORDER TO US:
getinfo@haworthpressinc.com

VISIT OUR WEB SITE AT:
http://www.HaworthPress.com

Take 20% Off Each Book! Special Sale

Order Today and Save!

TITLE	ISBN	REGULAR PRICE	20%-OFF PRICE

- Discount available only in US, Canada, and Mexico and not available in conjunction with any other offer.
- Individual orders outside US, Canada, and Mexico must be prepaid by check, credit card, or money order.
- In Canada: Add 7% for GST after postage & handling. Residents of Newfoundland, Nova Scotia, and New Brunswick, add an additional 8% for province tax.
- Outside USA, Canada, and Mexico: Add 20%.
- MN, NY, and OH residents: Add appropriate local sales tax.

Please complete information below or tape your business card in this area.

NAME _____

ADDRESS _____

_____

CITY _____

STATE _____ ZIP _____

COUNTRY _____

COUNTY (NY residents only) _____

TEL _____ FAX _____
[type or print clearly!]

E-MAIL _____
May we use your e-mail address for confirmations and other types of information?
( ) Yes ( ) No. We appreciate receiving your e-mail address and fax number. Haworth would like to e-mail or fax special discount offers to you, as a preferred customer. We will never **share, rent, or exchange** your e-mail address or fax number. We regard such actions as an invasion of your privacy.

POSTAGE AND HANDLING:
If your book total is: Add
up to $29.95 $5.00
$30.00 - $49.99 $6.00
$50.00 - $69.99 $7.00
$70.00 - $89.99 $8.00
$90.00 - $109.99 $9.00
$110.00 - $129.99 $10.00
$130.00 - $149.99 $11.00
$150.00 and up $12.00

- US orders will be shipped via UPS; Outside US orders will be shipped via Book Printed Matter. For shipments via other delivery services, contact Haworth for details. Based on US dollars. Booksellers: Call for freight charges. • If paying in Canadian funds, please use the current exchange rate to convert total to Canadian dollars. • Payment in UNESCO coupons welcome. • Please allow 3-4 weeks for delivery after publication.
- Prices and discounts subject to change without notice. • Discount not applicable on books priced under $15.00.

❑ **BILL ME LATER** ($5 service charge will be added).
(Bill-me option is not available on orders outside US/Canada/Mexico. Service charge is waived for booksellers/wholesalers/jobbers.)

Signature _____

❑ PAYMENT ENCLOSED _____
(Payment must be in US or Canadian dollars by check or money order drawn on a US or Canadian bank.)

❑ PLEASE CHARGE TO MY CREDIT CARD:
❑ AmEx ❑ Diners Club ❑ Discover ❑ Eurocard ❑ JCB ❑ Master Card ❑ Visa

Account # _____ Exp Date _____

Signature _____
May we open a confidential credit card account for you for possible future purchases? ( ) Yes ( ) No

(18) 12/00 BBC00

The Haworth Press, Inc
10 Alice Street, Binghamton, New York 13904-1580 USA